Praise for God Alone

God is always bigger and better than we think He is, however long we have been believers. This book will help enlarge our sense of God's power and His goodness, which makes it something every one of us needs. I found myself being wonderfully stretched and inspired.

SAM ALLBERRY
Pastor and author

Like J. I. Packer's classic *Knowing God*, this gem of a book combines deep theology, clearly explained, with searching pastoral application. Some doctrinal books lack pastoral application, and some pastoral works are weak on theological foundations. This book has both. My mind was expanded and my heart warmed. I warmly commend it.

CHRISTOPHER ASH
Writer-in-Residence, Tyndale House, Cambridge

"We do not know God as we should." This statement by Jonathan Griffiths might well be taken as the driving passion behind this book. The deep solution to many, if not most, of our problems, Griffiths argues, is knowing God in His various and glorious attributes. Although this argument is not in sync with the therapeutic and pragmatic *mentalité* of our age, an orientation that has impacted far too many sectors of Christianity, it is exactly what our churches need to hear and heed. Indeed, to this historian's ear, it is reminiscent of the Puritans, those skilled navigators of the seas of

Christian spirituality. And as the literature of those men and women did much good in the decades after their era, so I hope and pray that this book will bear much fruit in our day and those to come.

MICHAEL A. G. HAYKIN
Chair and professor of church history, The Southern Baptist Theological Seminary

Jonathan Griffiths has written a book that is both accessible and insightful. We need exactly this: a call to regain a vision of who the true God truly is. Read, and worship the God of the Bible.

JOSH MOODY
Senior pastor of College Church in Wheaton, IL, and the president and founder of God Centered Life Ministries

GOD ALONE

His Unique Attributes and How Knowing Them Changes Us

JONATHAN GRIFFITHS

MOODY PUBLISHERS

CHICAGO

Edited by Cheryl Molin and Jonathan Pountney
Interior design: Brandi Davis
Cover design: Derek Thornton / Notch Design
Cover illustration of crown copyright © 2022 by banyumilistudio / Shutterstock (1300849351). All rights reserved.

Library of Congress Cataloging-in-Publication Data

Names: Griffiths, Jonathan (Preaching instructor) author.
Title: God alone : his unique attributes and how knowing them changes us / Jonathan Griffiths.
Description: Chicago : Moody Publishers, [2022] | Includes bibliographical references. | Summary: "Our constant danger is that we have a view of God that is too small. With pastoral warmth and heart, Griffiths shows us God in all His beauty and goodness. Readers will gain knowledge of God›s attributes. Through this knowledge, trust, hope, and joy emerge. Confidence and faith grow stronger»-- Provided by publisher.
Identifiers: LCCN 2022029738 | ISBN 9780802473967 (paperback) | ISBN 9780802429032 (ebook)
Subjects: LCSH: God (Christianity)--Attributes.
Classification: LCC BT130 .G75 2022 | DDC 231/.4--dc23/eng/20220801
LC record available at https://lccn.loc.gov/2022029738

Originally delivered by fleets of horse-drawn wagons, the affordable paperbacks from D. L. Moody's publishing house resourced the church and served everyday people. Now, after more than 125 years of publishing and ministry, Moody Publishers' mission remains the same—even if our delivery systems have changed a bit. For more information on other books (and resources) created from a biblical perspective, go to www.moodypublishers.com or write to:

Moody Publishers
820 N. LaSalle Boulevard
Chicago, IL 60610

1 3 5 7 9 10 8 6 4 2

Printed in the United States of America

For Arabella

CONTENTS

ACKNOWLEDGMENTS

The substance of this book had its genesis in my Sunday preaching ministry at The Metropolitan Bible Church in Ottawa, Canada. I am grateful for a church family that is hungry for the Word of God and that delights in knowing God better. I was only able to undertake a teaching series that addressed subject matter of this kind because of the appetite of the congregation to be taught and to be stretched. I owe a debt of gratitude to the church family for their eagerness to learn and their patience to wrestle alongside me with these deep things of God. Our church eldership has encouraged me to consider writing a part of my ministry and kindly prompted me to persevere with the labor involved, trusting that the Lord might be pleased to use it for the good of others. This encouragement has made all the difference in causing this book to come to fruition.

I am thankful to Jonathan Pountney, who served both as my personal editor and literary agent for this project. His wisdom, creativity, and energy moved the project forward in a way that simply would not have been possible without him. It has been a joy to work with Trillia Newbell and her fine team at Moody Publishers. This book is markedly better thanks to their prompts, corrections, and suggestions for improvement. The process of working with the Moody team has reminded me once more of the great value of experienced publishers—especially Christian publishers—in producing books of quality and worth.

All of us who would teach or write stand on the shoulders of those who have taught us. During the course of this project, I have remembered with gratitude a number of gifted teachers who sought to give me a framework for understanding the doctrine of God during my undergraduate years at Oxford. More recently, my teachers have been authors whose works have stimulated and informed my mind, while also warming my heart. I cannot mention every author and every work that has informed this study on any level, but I would like to acknowledge the benefit I have received from contemporary works on the attributes of God by Matthew Barrett, Terry Johnson, and James Dolezal; the earlier devotional works of A. W. Pink and A. W. Tozer; and the numerous systematic theologies that have been richly beneficial throughout, not least those by Louis Berkhof, Wayne Grudem, Joel Beeke and Paul Smalley, and Michael Horton, to name a few. Often through these writers, I have been pointed to the treasures of Puritan reflection on the subject of God's attributes, and this has been of great benefit to me. Perhaps most refreshing and enriching of all has been the opportunity to interact with the thought of Thomas Watson. At various points I acknowledge key insights from these authors, but their influence and help are woven into this work throughout, and I would like to acknowledge with gratitude my debt to them at the outset.

Inevitably a project of this kind takes time, along with mental and spiritual energy. I am so thankful to my wife, Gemma, and our three children for bearing with me in seasons of busyness and times of distraction. They can quickly spot those moments when I am physically present but occupied by the thought of how best to reshape a paragraph or better frame an argument. I hope those times have been infrequent enough to be tolerable—but I know that grace has been required, and I am truly thankful to them.

It is my hope and prayer that this book, which I trust is faithful to God's Word in substance and spirit, will help readers to know Him better, to delight in Him, and thus to bring Him the glory that is His due.

introduction

THE ATTRIBUTES OF GOD

A ny competent doctor knows it is vital to look beyond symptoms to identify the root cause of any medical problem. Painkillers and bandages are never a cure, and yet the quick fix is attractive to doctor and patient alike. When we experience a wound or an ache, we gravitate toward treating the symptom quickly and moving on. The danger is, of course, that the underlying issue will never be addressed, with the result that the problem worsens and recurs.

In the Christian life, it is easy to focus on treating the symptoms of spiritual malaise without getting to the root cause. In churches and Christian books, blogs and broadcasts, much attention is given to such symptoms: the challenges of marriage, parenting, financial management, stress, overwork, conflict, addiction, and much more. The preacher, writer, or teacher knows that people will always have an appetite for material that speaks to those issues head-on.

But in producing and digesting material that focuses relentlessly on those themes, it is important for us to pause and ask whether we are not fixated on symptoms while ignoring the deeper cause of our difficulty.

As I reflect on my own Christian life, and on what I observe as a pastor within my own church, I have come to believe that a major source of difficulty and weakness in our personal discipleship and corporate church life is simply this: we do not know God as we should. We do not see Him as He is and we do not understand Him as He has made Himself known through His Word. In our me-focused world, where we are encouraged to fixate on our personal needs and wants to an almost obsessive degree, we readily give great attention to ourselves, while giving much less attention than we ought to the God who made us and who redeemed us in Christ. Our constant danger is that we have a view of God that is too small and domesticated, one formed from personal opinion and cultural assumption, rather than from the teaching of the Scriptures.

We do not need to read the Bible very long before we observe that the people of God run into very deep trouble when they do not know God properly. A lack of knowledge of God's power leads to a diminished trust in Him and His ability to save. A shallow knowledge of His holiness and worth leads to a lack of interest in serving and honoring Him. A diminished understanding of His love leads to a lack of confidence in His inclination to do us good. In all these ways and more, people who do not know God will fail to relate to Him properly and will end up in selfishness, faithlessness, and hopelessness.

The symptoms are familiar enough in our age as in every age. But we have not tended to focus on the root issue—that we do not know God well enough. A survey of theological and devotional literature on the theme of the attributes of God shows an intense interest in this theme among the Puritans of the seventeen and eighteenth century, but markedly less interest in it in popular evangelicalism since that time. There have been some notable exceptions, of course, including a heartening resurgence of interest in the doctrine of God Himself at the present time. This book is at once a plea that the people of God will know God better—and, at the same time, an invitation to those who do not yet know Him to come to know Him as He has revealed Himself in His Word.

Often theologians will divide the attributes of God into two groups (and will differ to some degree in the delineation of those groups). On the one hand are the "incommunicable" attributes of God; that is, the attributes that He does not share with (or "communicate to") His people. These attributes are unique to Him. On the other hand are the "communicable" attributes; that is, the attributes that God shares with (or "communicates to") His people. In this book, we focus on the incommunicable attributes of God. These attributes—like His omniscience and self-sufficiency—are true only of Him. The choice to begin here and focus here is intentional. I believe that we need to see God in His uniqueness and majesty and power before we can consider how He creates, redeems, calls, and enables us to be like Him in any way. God willing, I would like to consider the communicable attributes in another volume.

Theologians sometimes refer to the study of the doctrine of God as "theology proper." It is my prayer that this book of "theology proper" will feed your soul, raise your sights to the God who is so much higher and greater than we are, and then equip you to better know Him and serve Him.

one

THE ETERNAL GOD

I remember the sense, as a child, that the long summer holidays were never-ending. I have rather misty memories of sun-soaked days that ran one into the other. Once the thrill of liberation from school wore off a little, the prospect of many long days stretched ahead, perhaps with not enough activity to fill them, and a sense that they would never fully run their course. Inevitably, boredom set in at some point. Now, as an adult looking back on those long summer days, they seem to have come and gone in an instant— and I could wish to have even a few of them back.

Having the right perspective on time is important, both in ease and in trial. In both seasons, it is important to see that time is finite. We need to treasure the joys and endure the trials with patience. As adults, we look back on our childish perspective and wish we knew back then what we know now, but no amount of life experience will give us a fully mature perspective on time. Ultimately, to think rightly about time and to have the right perspective on the seasons of life we actually need the perspective of eternity. If we do not understand eternity—which is an attribute of God Himself—we will become over-immersed in our finite joys and over-burdened by our time-bound trials.

Psalm 90 opens with a resounding affirmation that the God of Israel is the eternal God. The God whom His people have known for generations is the God who has always been, "Before the mountains were brought forth, or ever you had formed the earth and the world, from everlasting to everlasting you are God" (v. 2). God's eternal being stands before and above the creation itself, and for Moses (who wrote the psalm), it is the eternity of God that gives the proper perspective on the brevity of life and on the suffering it brings. Having remembered the eternity of God, Moses turns to the brevity of the life of humanity, "The years of our life are seventy, or even by reason of strength eighty; yet their span is but toil and trouble" (v. 10). Moses then prays for the right perspective on time. A perspective, he says, that brings wisdom: "So teach us to number our days that we may get a heart of wisdom" (v. 12).

Moses was one who understood that the perspective of God's eternity makes sense of time and strengthens the people of God for trial and endurance. He had seen the people of God endure centuries of slavery in Egypt. He witnessed the long wait for their liberation as Pharaoh dragged his heels. And he experienced the decades of testing in the wilderness as they anticipated their entry into the promised land. Through all this, Moses's confidence was grounded in the eternity of God. He sought actively to instill that confidence in the people of Israel: "The eternal God is your dwelling place, and underneath are the everlasting arms" (Deut. 33:27). They, however, failed to learn the lesson. And the story of the wilderness wanderings is that of a people who did not endure trials in faith, at least in part because they did not grasp the eternity of God. Their trials were temporary, but God's people were in the hands of the God who always was and always will be—and so they could trust Him to carry them through and bring them to eternal dwellings.

The truth that Moses sought to teach the people is the consistent testimony of Scripture, "To the King of the ages, immortal, invisible, the only God, be honor and glory forever and ever" (1 Tim. 1:17); "I am the Alpha and the Omega . . . who is and who was and who is to come, the Almighty" (Rev. 1:8). God is eternal, the Scriptures teach us. But what does that really mean?

OUTSIDE OF TIME

At its core, God's eternity means that He is unbound and unlimited in relation to time. You and I are time-bound creatures, always living between an unchangeable past and an unknowable future. We are unlikely to often think about it, but it is essential to who we are. That is not so for God. Time is part of His creation, and as Maker of all things, He cannot be bound by time.[1]

Consider how the book of Genesis opens: "In the beginning God created . . ." It makes sense to assume that "the beginning" to which the writer refers is the beginning of time. It is, as it were, when the stopwatch starts rolling, and for that watch to move there needed to be the conditions that God established on the first day:

> And God said, "Let there be light," and there was light. And God saw that the light was good. And God separated the light from the darkness. God called the light Day, and the darkness he called Night. And there was evening and there was morning, the first day. (Gen. 1:3–5)

It takes days and nights, light and darkness, and the rotation of the earth for time to be counted. Time, as we understand it, only began with the creation events recorded here. And so, if time itself is part of God's creation, then His own existence as Creator must stand above and before the creation. His own eternal existence must be timeless itself.

The idea of time is actually something we struggle to grasp. By that I do not mean that some people are bad at timekeeping or poor at punctuality, but rather that all of us struggle to understand the notion of time and to articulate what it means. But as time-bound creatures, we struggle *all the more* with the notion of eternity. We cannot really imagine any kind of experience or reality that is not defined by time. The very concept almost overwhelms our rational capacity. Yet that is exactly who God is: He is eternal.

This is why God's eternity is central to our understanding of Him and why it is at the heart of His revelation of Himself. When Moses asked God how he should refer to Him before Pharaoh, the Lord said to him, "I AM WHO I AM" (Ex. 3:14). God is the Great I AM. There is nothing to add, nothing to take away. He is the absolute existence—no development, no change, no growth, no reduction. There is nothing relative about God. He is in no sense constrained. He simply *is*. Therefore, when God came to earth and entered human history through the incarnation, Jesus the Son of God declared this same identity for Himself. John recorded it clearly in his gospel, "Truly, truly, I say to you, before Abraham was, I am" (John 8:58). Abraham had a beginning, but before him, says Jesus, "I am." Absolute existence unbound by time.

Part of the reality of being time-bound creatures is that we experience everything in a progression. We move from one moment to another, encountering new things and new experiences all the time, and changing all the while as we pass through time. But it is not like that for the unchanging, eternal God. He, at once, holds time in its totality and sees history as a whole. God stands above time as the eternal One and as its Creator, but it is also true that He interacts with us *in* time. He is present and involved in the world, engaging with us as time-bound creatures. More than that, in the person of His Son, He has entered into human history. God speaks in history; reveals Himself in history; makes promises, gives warnings, responds to the sin and repentance of His people. He is patient in the unfolding of His will.

All that is true, but at the very same time, He remains the eternal One. The distinction between time and eternity is not something we can pin down very well, but various people have tried at least to illustrate it in some way. So, for instance, consider the difference between a river, through which water travels, and a lake, where it is held.[2] We experience our own existence in time as a river. Time flows, and we only see or touch part of it at any given moment. For us, time is never static. As Isaac Watts's great hymn puts it, "Time, like an ever-rolling stream, / bears all its sons away; / they fly, forgotten, as a dream / dies at the op'ning day."[3] In this sense, for us, time is a river.

For God, however, the whole of history is more like a lake or an ocean. He can see and comprehend the whole in a way that we never could in our finite existence. It is all there, gathered at once before His eternal gaze. When the Scriptures declare that He is the "Alpha and the Omega . . . the beginning and the end" (Rev. 22:13; see also Isa. 46:9–10), it is not simply that God was there at the beginning and will be there at the end. No; His eternity encompasses it all. He *is* the beginning and He *is* the end, even now.

Unlike us, God does not look back wistfully on the past. Neither is He consumed by the present or troubled by waiting for the future. He sees all of time as a vivid whole before His eyes: creation, the fall, the flood, the call of Abram, the monarchy, the exile, the incarnation, the early church, the medieval period, the Reformation, the World Wars, the technological progress of the twenty-first century, and much more besides. None of history is lost or filed away in the distant past. As the psalmist says, "A thousand years in your sight are but as yesterday when it is past, or as a watch in the night" (Ps. 90:4).

GIVING PERSPECTIVE TO THOSE OF US IN TIME

I do not pretend to be able to understand or fully conceptualize all of that—we all have huge limitations in our understanding of these things. Nonetheless, from what the Scriptures tell us, these things must be true of the God who made time, who is eternal, who never changes, and who knows the end from the beginning. If all this is true, what does it mean for His people? *What are the implications for us?*[4] There are, of course, many, but let me suggest four key implications. The first is that the eternity of God gives us *perspective*.

Notice again the outlook that the psalmist has on human life in light of God's eternity:

> You return man to dust
>   and say, "Return, O children of man!"
> For a thousand years in your sight
>   are but as yesterday when it is past,
>   or as a watch in the night.
>
> You sweep them away as with a flood; they are like a dream,
>   like grass that is renewed in the morning:
> in the morning it flourishes and is renewed;
>   in the evening it fades and withers. . . .
>
> The years of our life are seventy,
>   or even by reason of strength eighty;
> yet their span is but toil and trouble;
>   they are soon gone, and we fly away. . . .
>
> So teach us to number our days
>   that we may get a heart of wisdom. (Ps. 90:3–6, 10, 12)

His point is clear. We need the perspective of eternity if we are to live wisely in this world. The legendary businessman Warren

Buffett is one of the most successful investors in history. Buffett is quite an interesting character study on a number of levels, but if you know anything about him, you will know that at the very core of his genius is his long-term outlook. When asked his ideal time frame for holding an investment, his answer was simply, "Forever." Of course, companies and stocks will not last forever, and we know that full well. However, Buffett is able to make strategic investments that pay off handsomely because while the rest of the crowd is looking at what is happening today on Wall Street, Buffett is thinking about the prospects for a given company over the coming decades. His time frame is radically different from the average investor; that has been the key to his success. If we are consumed by the things that are immediately before us—the events going on around us today and the pleasures of the present time—if that is where our attention lies, we will make bad choices, unwise investments, and foolish mistakes. But as we consider our lives in light of the One who is eternal, we gain a heart of wisdom. That is what the psalmist saw.

In his first letter to the Corinthians, Paul gave a very intriguing exhortation. The immediate context is actually a discussion of marriage, but Paul wanted his readers to see that our perspective on everything in this world is shaped by the fact that this world is not eternal:

> This is what I mean, brothers: the appointed time has grown very short. From now on, let those who have wives live as though they had none, and those who mourn as though they were not mourning, and those who rejoice as though they were not rejoicing, and those who buy as though they had no goods, and those who deal with the world as though they had no dealings with it. For the present form of this world is passing away. (1 Cor. 7:29–31)

We are all naturally focused on the short term in our outlook, easily dazzled and consumed by the things immediately before us. But as we look upon the eternal God and hear His promises of a life to come, of heaven above, of a new creation in which we will live with Him, our eyes are lifted to see the bigger picture. His promises teach us to say no to the pleasures of sin, which are so fleeting, and no to the idols of this world, which will fade away. More than that, these realities also teach us to value knowing, loving, and serving the eternal God.

We all veer toward finding pleasure and fulfillment in the measly things immediately before us because we fail to lift our eyes to the bigger realities—the greater joys—that the Lord sets before us. The eternal God has spoken to us in His Word. He has entered our world in the person of His Son. He has invited us to receive eternal life and to join in His kingdom, which will have no end. By all this, in His grace He teaches us to number our days aright and He gives to us a heart of wisdom. The eternity of God gives us perspective.

SOVEREIGN OVER TIME

The second implication is that the eternity of God gives us *confidence* in God and His Word. For many of us, one of the most high-trust relationships in our lives is the relationship we have with our dentist. We need to trust and believe that the person who is allowed to wield needles and drills within our open mouth is competent, knowledgeable, and trustworthy. When my family moved to a new community some years ago, one priority for us was to find a good dentist. It just happened that the dentist closest to our house was someone with whom we had a family connection going back many years. He was well respected in the community and everyone was jostling to get on his list. He invited us in and we had our checkups. We were quickly persuaded he was the best dentist we had ever encountered. However, we had only been there a little more than a year when he told us that he was planning to retire. For the time he was our dentist we had a high-trust relationship, but it was a transient one.

Believers have no greater relationship of trust than our relationship with the Lord Himself. We take Him at His word, we stake our future on His promises, we entrust our very selves to Him for this life and the life to come. At the core of our willingness to do that is the belief that the One whom we trust can never cease to be. The One whom we trust has power over the future, so that His promises and His plans can never be frustrated.

All this is true, yet it is important to see that our confidence is not simply that God is *everlasting*, so that He will be around as long as time endures. No, our confidence goes further: it is that our God is the eternal God, the God who exists beyond time and holds time in His hand. You see, God's eternal nature teaches us that His plans are in no way subject to change or variation. He is the God who simply is. So, for instance, when He promises to save us at a final day, He sees that day already. That final day is, in some sense, present to Him now, and so His saving work is as good as complete.

Or, to look at it from another angle, when God accepts you into His family—when He sets His love upon you—His eternal nature means that His acceptance is in no way dependent upon your future performance. It is not as though He might change His mind if, down the road, you fail Him. No, when He saves you, He sees your life as a whole. He knows what you will do and what you will become. And despite all the future failings and sin that He knows are yet to come, He sets His love upon you. The present and future work of God are part of the coherent activity and reality of the eternal God who simply is. Later, in chapter 3, I will give more detail to the idea of God's unchanging nature

(His immutability), which is closely linked to this theme of God's eternal nature. But the glorious truth to meditate on for now is, as Hebrews says, that "Jesus Christ is the same yesterday and today and forever" (Heb. 13:8).

I recently came across a news article with the reassuring heading, "Why the Canada Pension Plan Will Still Be Solvent When You Retire." In a world of depressing news stories, it was a very nice headline to read and, no doubt, many of the article's readers will take comfort in it. We can all have those niggling doubts that our future financial plans will fail us. Plenty of company pension pots have been raided; plenty of retirement plans have run out of money; and the truth is that anything can happen. But when we trust ourselves to the eternal God who does not change—who is the same God now who holds the end of time in His hand—we know that the future is secure and we can stake everything on His promises. Scripture proclaims the supremely comforting truth that "The eternal God is your dwelling place, and underneath are the everlasting arms" (Deut. 33:27). Here is our security for time and for eternity; here is our refuge in the storms of life, our sure and steadfast hope: we know One who is eternal and whose arms beneath us are everlasting. The eternity of God gives us confidence.

SOVEREIGN OVER ETERNITY

The third implication is that the eternity of God gives us a *warning*. Psalm 90 asks, "Who considers the power of your anger, and your wrath according to the fear of you?" (v. 11). As the psalmist reflected on the sheer immensity of the eternal God, he naturally exclaimed that God is capable of wrath appropriate to His majesty. Of course, when we examine the Bible honestly, we see that this is true. We see that the eternal God is capable of wrath that does not end.

If I were to take a poll to find the most unpopular Christian doctrine of all, I think there would be very little competition: the doctrine of the everlasting punishment of the wicked is surely the least popular and the most despised teaching in the Bible. When we do wrong and cause hurt and offense in human relationships, we hope that the storm will pass, the injury fade, and the wrongdoing be forgotten. Similarly, when it comes to sin before God, we might hope that the passing of time will make our wrongdoing smaller in His sight. But the eternal God sees all of history before Him. Psalm 90 reminds us that the eternal God sees all our sin before His eyes, "For we are brought to an end by your anger; by your wrath we are dismayed. You have set our iniquities before you, our secret sins in the light of your presence" (vv. 7–8).

The Puritan Thomas Watson wrote that the eternity of God is "thunder and lightning to the wicked," and that "God lives for ever; and as long as God lives he will be punishing the damned."[5] The Bible makes it abundantly clear that this is true. No one is more frank about the matter than Jesus Himself. In the parable of the sheep and the goats he says, "Then he [the King] will say to those on his left, 'Depart from me, you cursed, into the eternal fire prepared for the devil and his angels'" (Matt. 25:41). And again, "If your eye causes you to sin, tear it out. It is better for you to enter the kingdom of God with one eye than with two eyes to be thrown into hell, 'where their worm does not die and the fire is not quenched'" (Mark 9:47–48). The God who judges sin lives forever and His enemies will never reach the day where they can escape His judgments.

This is a sobering, even frightening, thought. At the same time, it is a truth that we need to reckon with in a serious way. Perhaps you are someone who would call yourself a Christian, but you know that you are denying the Lord by your lifestyle and rejecting Him by embracing sin. You might be living in active defiance against Him. If so, let me urge you and plead with you to consider what it really means to turn away from the eternal God and to face His unending wrath. Again, Thomas Watson drove home the force of this truth:

> Thoughts of eternal torments are a good antidote against sin. Sin tempts us with pleasure; but, when we think of eternity, it may cool the intemperate heat of lust. Shall I, for the pleasure of sin for a season, endure eternal pain? . . . Is sin committed so sweet as lying in hell for ever is bitter? This thought would make us flee from sin.[6]

One of my pastor friends sometimes shares the story of going to see a member of his congregation who was pursuing an adulterous relationship. He was set on leaving his wife for another woman. My friend pleaded with him not to do it, but the man gave him the most harrowing reply, "I would prefer to go to hell than give up this relationship." The man knew enough of God's Word to know the nature of the choice he was making. He was rejecting the Word of God—he was willfully defying the eternal Judge—and he was embracing a punishment that would not end.

Reader, if you are living in rebellion against God and holding on to some sin that you know defies Him, if you are not submitting your life to Him, let me plead with you to simply consider the reality of God's eternity. What could be more important? What could be more urgent? And if you have not yet turned to Christ for forgiveness, let me plead with you as well: take seriously the warnings of the Bible and do not risk the judgment of the eternal God.

THE HOPE FOUND IN THE ETERNITY OF GOD

If the eternity of God gives us perspective, confidence, and a warning, then it also, finally and briefly, gives us *hope*. C. S. Lewis writes of the "surprise" of the passing of time, "Notice how we are perpetually *surprised* at Time. ('How time flies! Fancy John being grown-up and married? I can hardly believe it!') In heaven's name, why? Unless, indeed, there is something in us which is *not* temporal."[7]

Most of us have experienced surprise at the passing of time. Something within us even mourns it. It means getting older, it means change, and it often means loss. The Scriptures tell us why we feel this way. We find the passing of time hard because "he has put eternity into man's heart" (Eccl. 3:11). We feel we were not made to die and we long for eternity. We long for life that lasts and for a reality that will endure beyond this passing world and its variation, loss, and decay. We all know that longing. And the answer to it is not found in the sports car or plastic surgery of the midlife crisis. It is not found in success or wealth or fame. It is not found anywhere in this world. It is found only in the eternal God who holds time in His hand. You and I had a beginning and we are bound by time. But here is what we can do in the face of our temporality: we can know and relate to the eternal God who has the power to give us life that will not end. Jesus tells us that eternal life is tied to knowing the eternal God. "And this is eternal life," he says, "that they know you, the only true God, and Jesus Christ whom you have sent" (John 17:3).

The eternal God came into the world in the person of His Son, who gave His life to pay the debt of our sin that we might be set free from the judgment of sin and the terror of hell and be released for an endless future of joy with Him. The promises of God are great; the warnings of God are terrible. But for us who know Him, He is our dwelling place, our refuge, and our eternal hope.

two

THE OMNIPOTENT GOD

M ost evenings one of our children begins his prayers by
thanking God that He, God, is more powerful than anyone
else. The supreme power of God is, if you like, the foundation of his
theology. It is a very good foundation. If we do not believe that God
is all-powerful, we do not believe that He is God at all. Some of the
most wonderful reflections on the sheer power of God anywhere in
Scripture are found in the book of Job, and I can think of no better
way to begin this second chapter than by quoting Job:

> "The dead tremble
>   under the waters and their inhabitants.
> Sheol is naked before God,
>   and Abaddon has no covering.
> He stretches out the north over the void
>   and hangs the earth on nothing.

He binds up the waters in his thick clouds,
　　and the cloud is not split open under them. . . .
He has inscribed a circle on the face of the waters
　　at the boundary between light and darkness.
The pillars of heaven tremble
　　and are astounded at his rebuke.
By his power he stilled the sea;
　　by his understanding he shattered Rahab.
By his wind the heavens were made fair;
　　his hand pierced the fleeting serpent.
Behold, these are but the outskirts of his ways,
　　and how small a whisper do we hear of him!
　　But the thunder of his power who can understand?"
(Job 26:5–8, 10–14)

Who, then, can understand the thunder of the power of Almighty God? The answer, of course, is that none of us fully can. In great displays of His power in the created order, all we see, says Job, is the outer fringe of His work ("outskirts" in the ESV). What a thought. Our perception of the extent and greatness of His power is so limited, and it certainly is too small. The aim of this chapter is to try to expand our view of the power of God toward a more biblical proportion and catch even a glimpse of His might from the pages of His Word.

　　The reason we need this big view of God's power is not simply so that our theology will be correct—as important as that is—but so that our hearts will rest secure in Him. The simple fact is that if our view of God's power is too small, we will not trust Him. We will not trust Him as we should in the good times and we certainly will not trust Him in the hard times. And perhaps that is precisely where you are. Hard times have come and you are wondering: Has God lost His grip on the situation? Have the waves of this raging sea not only overwhelmed me, but have they actually overwhelmed *Him?*

Perhaps you have had the unsettling experience of going down a zip line. Whether you have or not, you can picture the setup: a wire suspended between a high point at one end and a lower point off in the distance. You put on a harness that has wheeled pulley clips attached to the wire and you go flying down. When you first get wired up to the zip line, your instinct is to hold on to something solid—you want to grip the main suspension wire at the top. But the instructor warns you not to do that because you will shred your hand if you try. You need to believe that the harness that is fitted to you is strong enough to hold you on the line. You need to have confidence. It is like that when considering the power of God. We need to have absolute confidence in Him if we are to trust Him properly and avoid shredding our hands by trying to take hold of the situation ourselves.

The Bible gives us ample warning of the dangers of having too small a view of God and His power when the pressure rises and difficulty comes our way. We see it in the life of Abraham and Sarah, who, facing childlessness, chose to take matters into their own hands by seeking a child through Hagar, Sarah's maid, with disastrous results (Gen. 16). We see it with the Israelites in the exodus generation. As God delivered the people from Egypt and took them out into the wilderness, they immediately doubted His power to provide and to protect. At the first pang of hunger, the people became convinced that they would be left to starve to death. So they grumbled against Moses, "Would that we had died by the hand of the Lord in the land of Egypt, when we sat by the meat pots and ate bread to the full, for you have brought us out into this wilderness to kill this whole assembly with hunger" (Ex. 16:3). When they came to the threshold of the promised land and sent in spies to survey the scene, and when the report came back of its powerful inhabitants, the people cried out, wept, and grumbled, "Would that we had died in the land of Egypt! Or would that we had died in this wilderness! Why is the Lord bringing us into this land, to fall by the sword?" (Num. 14:2–3). The Lord heard their faithless grumbling, and the result was that the entire adult generation who grumbled was barred entry to the land, and the people wandered forty years in the wilderness. It was, at its heart, a failure to trust in the power of God.

GOD'S POWER OVER CREATION

The theme for this chapter is the *omnipotence* of God—the truth that He is all-powerful and that He can do anything that accords with His character and will. The Bible teaches us again and again that God is all-powerful, reigning as sovereign over the universe. As Job rightly said to God, "I know that you can do all things, and that no purpose of yours can be thwarted" (Job 42:2), or as the angel Gabriel said to Mary, "nothing will be impossible with God" (Luke 1:37). Of course, to consider all the ways in which God's power is made manifest in the universe would take a book with a broader range and scope than this one, so I want to focus on four areas where God's power is seen in the universe, and the first is in *creation*.

I understand that one of the largest construction projects currently underway anywhere in the world is the great south-north water transfer project in China. The north of China has a huge population but a limited supply of water, so the government has decided that the solution is to take water from the south through three massive canals, each more than six hundred miles long. The project is scheduled to take forty-eight years to complete and is projected to deliver about forty-five billion cubic meters of water to the north each year. It is an impressive project, a reshaping of the landscape and the environment on a massive scale, and a stunning display of logistical and financial power.

Yet consider the power of God made manifest in creation: the great mountains, the oceans, the islands, the continents, the soaring sky, the beautiful and diverse creatures, and humanity itself. And that is just planet Earth. Consider the universe: the stars, the planets, and countless galaxies. I understand that the visible universe is about ninety-three billion light-years in diameter at the present time. That is far bigger than any of us can begin to contemplate. Then consider the fact that God made the universe by the power of His word. He spoke, and it came into being. One moment there was nothing; the next moment worlds were born. No laborers, no machines, no fundraising, no logistical analyses. Just a word and worlds were born. Can we even fathom that kind of power?

It is one thing to make something; it is quite another to run and maintain it. The world's landscape is dotted with grand projects that are either unfinished or abandoned. Perhaps the most famous of these is North Korea's Ryugyong Hotel. The 330-meter tall giant has towered over Pyongyang since 1987, when construction began. The building is officially still "under construction," but it is essentially abandoned. The reality is that the huge project was more than the state could manage to complete or sustain.

In the first chapter of Hebrews we are told that Jesus the Son of God "is the radiance of the glory of God and the exact imprint of his nature, and he upholds the universe by the word of his power" (Heb. 1:3). Paul expressed the same thought in Colossians when he wrote, "He is before all things, and in him all things hold together" (Col. 1:17). The point is that not only has God made the universe, but He upholds it moment by moment. Were God to cease upholding us by the word of His power, the universe itself would tear apart at the seams. It would disintegrate and we would cease to be.

God is the Almighty, the King of creation. How should we respond to Him? At the most fundamental level, God's power in creating and sustaining us and our world means that we owe Him our obedience and our worship. That may appear to be an obvious point, but it takes us to the fundamental question at the heart of the gospel, a question that all unbelievers ask on some level: Why should anyone submit to the lordship of Jesus Christ? After all, when we declare the gospel message, that is precisely what we are calling people to do. The offer of salvation is wonderful, but why is it that we owe God allegiance and worship?

Simply put, we are His creatures, and our very existence depends upon Him. Each breath is a gift and each moment of existence is a sign of His kindness. To refuse to honor Him, thank Him, and worship Him is therefore not simply discourteous, but wicked. This is a point that Paul develops in a very important passage at the beginning of the book of Romans:

> For the wrath of God is revealed from heaven against all ungodliness and unrighteousness of men, who by their unrighteousness suppress the truth. For what can be known about God is plain to them, because God has shown it to them. For his invisible attributes, namely, his eternal power and divine nature, have been clearly perceived, ever since the creation of the world, in the things that have been made. So they are without excuse. For although they knew God, they did not honor him as God or give thanks to him, but they became futile in their thinking, and their foolish hearts were darkened. (Rom. 1:18–21)

To refuse to thank and worship God for His power and kindness in creation is a serious thing. If you cannot, for the life of you, figure out why you should bother with God, why He has any right to say to you how you should live your life, here is the reason: He made you. If you are struggling to articulate the gospel to a friend or family member and you do not know where to start, then start with the fact of creation. God made us, and so we owe Him our allegiance. That is why sin is a problem. That is why God has a right to hold us to account. That is why we need saving from His judgment. God's power is expressed in the creation and, actually, that is the foundation of everything.

GOD'S POWER OVER HISTORY

If God's power is seen in creation, then it is also true that God's power is seen in history. Of course, it can sometimes feel as though history is spinning out of control. We look around the world and see corrupt governments making life difficult for their people and tensions rising between nations. Politicians lose their grip on power and leaders are deposed, yet other corrupt leaders take their place. As we look on at our chaotic world order, the Scriptures tell us that rulers and nations operate within the sovereign power of God, "The king's heart is a stream of water in the hand of the Lord; he turns it wherever he will" (Prov. 21:1). Living in exile, Daniel declared to Nebuchadnezzar (the ruler of the greatest superpower of the day) that power was only his because God gave it to him. "The God of heaven has given the kingdom, the power, and the might, and the glory," he said. "He has given, wherever they dwell, the children of man, the beasts of the field, and the birds of the heavens, making you rule over them all" (Dan. 2:37–38). In New Testament times, when the godless Roman Empire dominated the world order, Paul expressed the same belief, "Let every person be subject to the governing authorities. For there is no authority except from God, and those that exist have been instituted by God" (Rom. 13:1).

As we look at the world today from our own vantage point, it is easy to be concerned about the direction things are taking. We may fear what the future holds. Yet the Bible comforts us by teaching us that no government is established unless the sovereign God establishes it. His power extends to the world of governance as it does to everything else. This does not mean that all the things that governments do are pleasing to God and in line with His Word. No, sometimes governments commit great evil. But the comfort is that no government can overwhelm the power of God and no turn in human history happens apart from His sovereign control.

When I was a child my favorite ride at the theme park was a racing car that I got to drive myself. Perhaps you have been on a ride like this. You get into the little car (which runs on a lawnmower engine), you have an accelerator and steering wheel and, for all intents and purposes, you are driving. What you do not quite realize when you are five years old, however, is that a metal ridge runs all the way along the track underneath your car and your wheels cannot cross it; you cannot deviate from your lane. You can steer within the limits, you can experience a sense of freedom and power, but you cannot leave your lane.

There is a real sense in which human rulers and governments are placed in a lane to which God has assigned them. They feel powerful—and, to be sure, they wield true power—but they serve only within the limits that God's power allows. Of course, you and I need to know and understand this if we are going to sleep at night and have any peace about the future. The rise and fall of governments and nations only happens within the sovereignty of God. What will happen in upcoming elections? What about tensions with China, Iran, North Korea, and Russia? The sovereign God knows and He has it covered. We must not be anxious, but we must pray and trust the sovereign Lord of all to direct the affairs of human history in accordance with His will.

The fact that God's power is seen in world history is a wonderful truth, but it naturally raises a question: What about the forces of evil in the world? If God is good and God is powerful, then what about when bad things happen, when evil rulers rise, when cruelty is unleashed, when events unfold that are so clearly not good? What then about the power of God?

GOD'S POWER OVER EVIL

So far, none of the things we have thought about in this chapter will have come as much of a surprise. God's power is expressed in creation and in history. These facts are familiar to the believer. But this next area where we see God's power at work could come as something of a surprise, for the Bible shows us that God's power is seen over the forces of evil.

In thinking about this, we enter into some of the more perplexing and challenging teaching of the Scriptures. If we are committed to reading our Bibles, we will encounter incidents from time to time when God clearly exercised His power over the forces of evil and sometimes in situations that seem pretty perplexing on first reading. The most familiar incident along those lines is the encounter between Joseph and his brothers many years after they sold him into slavery in Egypt. Joseph had, through a series of God-ordained events, been exalted to a position from which he was able to save his people from famine. You may remember the famous words that Joseph spoke to his brothers, "You meant evil against me, but God meant it for good, to bring it about that many people should be kept alive, as they are today" (Gen. 50:20). The brothers were working evil and acting with malice and cruelty, but God had a bigger plan—a good plan—and the brothers were unwittingly participating in it.

The incident is famous and familiar to many, but to fully understand the depth of this truth, it is useful to consider a less familiar and, in some ways, much stranger example. Later in Israel's history, King Ahab wanted to go to war against Ramoth Gilead. However, before he committed to battle he wanted the prophets to affirm him in his decision. He had a whole crowd of false prophets who did that, but one prophet of the Lord called Micaiah did not fall into line. King Ahab was frustrated, and so Micaiah delivered this message to him:

> "Therefore hear the word of the LORD: I saw the LORD sitting on his throne, and all the host of heaven standing beside him on his right hand and on his left; and the LORD said, 'Who will entice Ahab, that he may go up and fall at Ramoth-gilead?' And one said one thing, and another said another. Then a spirit came forward and stood before the LORD, saying, 'I will entice him.' And the LORD said to him, 'By what means?' And he said, 'I will go out, and will be a lying spirit in the mouth of all his prophets.' And he said, 'You are to entice him, and you shall succeed; go out and do so.'" (1 Kings 22:19–22)

I do not know what you make of this incident, but I think that is more or less the strangest Bible story I have ever read. We are given a view into the throne room of heaven, the hosts of heaven are gathered before God, and a consultation is taking place: *Any ideas on how to deal with Ahab? How to entice him into this battle?* Then, perhaps, one idea from the back of the room . . . *No, that will not work.* Another idea from an angel in the front row . . . *No, that is too obvious.* We can only imagine how the meeting went. The scene is remarkable. But a mysterious figure over in the corner pipes up (this may well be Satan himself speaking), "How about if I go and be a lying spirit in the mouths of the prophets and tell him that the battle will go well for him? How about that idea?" And the Lord says: *That will work. Go and do it.* The Lord sends a lying spirit to go and put lies into the mouths of the prophets to entice the king to his death. (It is important to see that he also sent His true prophet to speak the truth. This is a test for Ahab.)

It is all so strange to our eyes. You could not make this up; and it raises a lot of tricky questions for us, some of which we will not be able to answer. But, despite all the questions it raises, this incident demonstrates to us that God has power over the forces of evil, and is willing and able to use those forces to achieve His greater purpose. God had purposed to bring judgment against the ungodly King Ahab, and ultimately He used these lying spirits to reveal and confirm Ahab's disdain for God's work and send him into a battle where he was killed. God's good and righteous purpose was achieved, but the agency was evil and not good. However odd and perplexing that is to our eyes, it is actually a great comfort. It means that no forces can operate beyond and outwit God or His decree. He is truly sovereign. He is truly almighty.

The greatest example of this principle, of course, is found at the cross of Christ. In the crucifixion of the Son of God we see the most wicked event in the history of the world. Here is the full ugliness of sin and human rebellion unmasked. Here is wickedness in all its fury let loose on the righteous One. Here, it would seem, is Satan unleashed. But listen to the way the apostle Peter spoke of the event afterward in the book of Acts. Speaking to the people of Judea he declared one of the most theologically loaded sentences in the whole of the Bible, "This Jesus, delivered up according to the definite plan and foreknowledge of God, you crucified and killed by the hands of lawless men" (Acts 2:23). What a statement. Just let that sink in for a moment. The most wicked event in the history of the world happened by the set purpose and foreknowledge of God. We know that the Father had a glorious and righteous plan for the death of Jesus, a plan for the forgiveness of our sin and for our salvation. And yet the murder of Jesus itself was an evil act committed by evil people, "you crucified and killed [Him] by the hands of lawless men." The wicked men are fully responsible. What they did was evil. But all of it happened under and within the sovereign power and plan of God.

Here we bump firmly against one of the great mysteries of Scripture: How can God be truly God Almighty, with power extending to the governance of all things—evil people and evil spirits included—and yet, at the same time, be entirely good and righteous? I cannot pretend to solve the conundrum. There is real mystery here. The Bible affirms both things to be true. God is in charge in this world. He is entirely good and never does evil. In thinking this through we need to recognize that God's sovereignty over good and evil function differently. They are not symmetrical. That is, when it comes to achieving good and righteous things, God does them directly. He sends His Holy Spirit and He speaks His Word and He blesses His people. He does these things Himself. But when it comes to evil, God does not *do* these things, but gives limited freedom for evil spirits and evil people to do them. He is not doing them Himself but He allows them, and sometimes, as we have seen, even sends others who do them.

By all accounts, that is a lot to process and is perhaps more than we can fully digest. To return to our commonplace world for just a moment, it is like going to a buffet restaurant and reaching a point that you realize you have got more on your plate than you can really manage to deal with in a dignified way. Similarly, I think we reach that point mentally and spiritually with this concept, but (and this is where the analogy with the buffet ends) it is good for us to give it a try and to think about it. This fulsome doctrine of the sovereignty of God is a wonderful doctrine for us to hold because it means that God has the power to set boundaries around evil. Even though we have chosen sin and welcomed the destruction of the fall into this world, and even though we are responsible for so much evil, God has graciously limited our experience of evil, so that we do not feel its full force.

Moreover, we see here that God is at work in all things to accomplish His good purposes for His people and His world. Many of us will be familiar with Romans 8:28, "And we know that for those who love God all things work together for good, for those who are called according to his purpose." It is a verse to cling to in times of difficulty. It is a wonderful verse, but we can only believe that God is at work in all things—evil, painful, and tragic things included—if we believe that His power extends to them and is sovereign over them. It is a challenging truth but a vitally important one. God's power is seen over the forces of evil.

GOD'S POWER THROUGH THE GOSPEL

Finally and supremely, we see God's power at work through the gospel. A little while ago I was in an electronics store looking at some new generation Bluetooth speakers. I tried out some of the really mini ones, pressed "Play" on the test button, and could not believe the sound that came out. Despite its scale and appearance, it produced enough sound to fill the huge warehouse store.

At the opening of his great letter to the Romans, Paul set out his confidence in the gospel. It so often seems like a small and weak thing, but Paul knew it contains extraordinary power. "I am not ashamed of the gospel, for it is the power of God for salvation to everyone who believes" (Rom. 1:16). The gospel message proclaimed is the power of the almighty God to save lost and dying people and bring the spiritually dead back to spiritual life. Elsewhere, in Ephesians, Paul wrote of "the immeasurable greatness of his [God's] power toward us who believe." He went on, "according to the working of his great might that he worked in Christ when he raised him from the dead and seated him at his right hand in the heavenly places" (Eph. 1:19–20). God powerfully raised Jesus from the dead and raised Him on high. That was the miracle of all miracles, and Paul told us that that same power is at work in the people of God, in gospel people, in *us*. That power is at work by the Spirit to transform us, grow us in godliness, and enable us to serve Him.

God is able to do all things. Often I think that what we need to be convinced of most is not that God will work out His wider purposes for the world in accordance with His will, or that He will continue to uphold creation, or bring about the ultimate consummation of His kingdom, but rather that God's power will actually be enough to sustain us, enable us, and energize us for godliness, ministry, and service. This is the point at which practical atheism can set in for many. We may believe the big headline truths about God. We may believe that He is eternal and holy and just and omniscient and omnipotent—at least when it comes to the big things in the world—but it may be that you believe that your personal situation is such that His power is not enough. It may be that you believe that you are actually beyond the salvation of God. You may believe that God is all-powerful in theory, but that you are un-savable in practice; that your sin is too great; you've wandered too far; your life is too messy.

I would not be surprised at all if there is someone reading this book who feels that way. But if you do, take this truth to heart: God really is the Almighty One. He is the doctor of the soul for whom no patient is too far gone. His power through the gospel is sufficient to bring life and transformation, if only you will respond to Jesus Christ in repentance and faith. For others—perhaps most readers—you have been saved and you do belong to Christ, but you may struggle to believe in the power of God when it comes to living the Christian life, when it comes to battling sin, when it comes to finding strength to serve and keep on serving, when it comes to discouragement and the temptation to give up following and trusting Jesus. Flinging stars into space by the word of His mouth—*no problem.* Getting me through this time of temptation, family conflict, difficulty at church—*I am not so sure.*

I expect we all know something of that. We feel worn down and discouraged. We are aware of our failure and our sin and we wonder if we can continue. The apostle Paul had that kind of experience. He wrote about it movingly in his second letter to the church in Corinth:

> So to keep me from becoming conceited because of the surpassing greatness of the revelations, a thorn was given me in the flesh, a messenger of Satan to harass me, to keep me from becoming conceited. Three times I pleaded with the Lord about this, that it should leave me. But he said to me, "My grace is sufficient for you, for my power is made perfect in weakness." Therefore I will boast all the more gladly of my weaknesses, so that the power of Christ may rest upon me. For the sake of Christ, then, I am content with weaknesses, insults, hardships, persecutions, and calamities. For when I am weak, then I am strong.
> (2 Cor. 12:7–10)

Like Paul, we need to believe that the omnipotent God is powerfully at work through His Spirit, and His strength is more than sufficient for weak people like us. We need to believe that His great power is sufficient for every challenge and trial we face; sufficient for every surprise and change of plan we encounter; sufficient for every task and ministry He calls us to undertake. God is the all-powerful One—powerful over creation, history, evil—and gloriously powerful through the gospel, by His Spirit, in His people.

three

THE UNCHANGING GOD

We live on the southern outskirts of our city, and we are finding these days that almost every time we drive north into town the landscape has changed. A new apartment complex goes up. New ground gets turned over for a fresh subdivision. Our city is in a time of constant and relentless change. It feels energizing and exciting on one level, but there is also something a little destabilizing about it too.

When we lived in the UK we always enjoyed visiting places that seemed immune to change—rural villages, castles, and countryside—where things have been more or less the same for as long as anyone can remember. Despite the variations of the years, the places that we visited had not changed much in a long time. I think everyone, to some degree, loves those fixed points in life. They are comforting to us because we live in a rapidly changing world. We ourselves are constantly changing and developing even though, not to be too morbid about it, we are actually constantly declining as we move through each day.

The psalmist spoke of this experience in Psalm 102, "For my days pass away like smoke, and my bones burn like a furnace" (v. 3). And again later on, "My days are like an evening shadow; I wither away like grass" (v. 11). It was the psalmist's reality, and it is still ours. Even the world itself deteriorates. The psalmist cut to the heart of the issue: "Of old you laid the foundation of the earth, and the heavens are the work of your hands." He went on, "They will perish, but you will remain; they will all wear out like a garment. You will change them like a robe, and they will pass away" (vv. 25–26). We are changing and declining; our world is changing and will not last. But the psalmist proclaimed the glorious truth that God does not change, "But you, O LORD, are enthroned forever; you are remembered throughout all generations," and against the background of our world's perishing, "but you are the same, and your years have no end" (Ps. 102:12, 27).

The Scriptures could not be clearer. The Lord is the unchanging One. All else will change and decay and much will disappear, but the eternal God does not change. The nineteenth-century hymn writer Walter Chalmers Smith captured this sentiment so well, "We blossom and flourish as leaves on the tree, / and wither and perish but nought changeth thee."[1] The Bible affirms this truth again and again, "I the Lord do not change; therefore you, O children of Jacob, are not consumed" (Mal. 3:6); "Every good gift and every perfect gift is from above, coming down from the Father of lights, with whom there is no variation or shadow due to change" (James 1:17); "Jesus Christ is the same yesterday and today and forever" (Heb. 13:8). In fact, the name by which God introduced Himself to Moses, the name "I Am," carries with it the truth that God does not change. He is the One who was and is and is to come—always the same—simply the "I Am." The unchangeability (or "immutability") of God is a wonderful Bible truth. That God does not change is basic orthodoxy that Christians have understood and affirmed throughout church history. But what does it mean for us that God is immutable, and what are the implications? Well, in the first place it means that *His character does not change.*

GOD'S UNCHANGING CHARACTER

It is awful to have to interact with a fickle person, someone prone to changing their mind. You never know what a day will bring. If that person is in a position of authority over you, it can be a fearful thing to have to engage with them. In a discussion of challenging workplace dynamics, Lynn Taylor explained, "It can be disconcerting to start the morning with a cheery, angelic boss, only to find that by 4 p.m. he has morphed into the creature from the Black Lagoon."[2] Personally, I am grateful that I have not had to experience that myself, but maybe it strikes a chord with you. The point is this: the immutability of God means that we know how God will be and how He will interact with us and treat us. He never has bad days. He never wakes up on the wrong side of the bed. As His people, we are not subject to divine whims and mood swings. He will treat us today as He has always treated His people.

That is the point the writer of Hebrews made in chapter 13 of his letter. He began by encouraging the readers to imitate their leaders in the way they walk with the Lord, "Remember your leaders, those who spoke to you the word of God. Consider the outcome of their way of life, and imitate their faith" (Heb. 13:7). The idea is to reflect on how it went for them trusting and following Jesus. It went well; they finished strong. The implication is that if it went well for them, then it will go well for you, too. And the basis of that claim is that "Jesus Christ is the same yesterday and today and forever" (Heb. 13:8). Jesus Christ never changes. He will behave toward you as He did toward believers who have gone before. He will be gracious and kind and forgiving and persevering and sustaining. He will be all the things He always is to His people.

Sometimes you can have the frustrating experience of taking a recommendation from friends that turns out badly—perhaps a restaurant to try, a hotel to stay in, a car to buy, or a school to attend. They had a fabulous experience in the past, they tell you, but when you try the same thing it is a disaster. Why is that? Well, sometimes it is because the company has changed and the organization has gone downhill. It is not what it once was.

In his great song recorded in Deuteronomy 32, Moses declared this about the Lord:

> For I will proclaim the name of the LORD;
> ascribe greatness to our God!
>
> "The Rock, his work is perfect,
> for all his ways are justice.
> A God of faithfulness and without iniquity,
> just and upright is he." (Deut. 32:3–4)

God is the rock, the One on whom we can depend. Big rocks do not tend to move or change very much year by year, and the image points us to the stability and trustworthiness of our unchanging God. In a world like ours, how much we need to know the One who does not change and the One on whom we can rely. It may be that you are looking for some kind of stability in a time of chaos or disappointment or grief or overwhelming change. Maybe you are searching for something stable and dependable in a confusing and changeable world. Well, this is the God in whom we trust, and He offers each one of us security, stability, and steadfast love if we come to Him through Jesus Christ. God's character is unchanging.

J. C. Ryle, in the introduction to his book *Holiness*, wrote, "I have had a deep conviction for many years that practical holiness and entire self-consecration to God are not sufficiently attended to. . . . Politics, or controversy, or party spirit, or worldliness, have eaten out the heart of lively piety in too many of us." He went on with concern for nineteenth-century Christians who had lost their biblical vision for holiness. "The subject of personal godliness has fallen sadly into the background. The standard of living has become painfully low in many quarters. The immense importance of 'adorning the doctrine of God our Savior' (Titus 2:10), and making it lovely and beautiful by our daily habits and tempers, has been far too much overlooked."[3] Reflecting on those comments, I often wonder what Ryle, if he were transported here to observe our lives, would make of us today. I wonder what would strike him about our standards of holiness.

GOD'S UNCHANGING STANDARDS

No doubt we would look on some of the exhortations that Ryle sets out in his book as antiquated and even a little strange. It is quite common for one generation of Christians to look on the habits and standards of a former generation and revise them or set them aside. Ryle saw it in his day, and we see it in ours. But we need to be careful: the fact that God is unchanging means, second, that His *standards are unchanging*, too. What the immutable God says is right in one age is right in every age, and what He says is wrong in one age is always wrong. The psalmist again makes this clear, "Forever, O LORD, your word is firmly fixed in the heavens. Your faithfulness endures to all generations; you have established the earth, and it stands fast. By your appointment they stand this day" (Ps. 119:89–91). The words of the immutable God are unchanging. His laws endure. Of course, certain practices in the Old Testament (temple regulations, dietary and hygiene laws, and more) served to point God's people forward to Christ, and were then fulfilled and set aside with His arrival. However, the moral law of God does not change. The Ten Commandments are not up for revision or renegotiation every few years.

This is very important for us to consider and reflect upon because the winds of change are blowing strongly in our culture and we are more shaped by our context than we can ever know or realize. We do not want to live in a subcultural bubble, but we have to keep evaluating the values that we imbibe through institutions and media and ask ourselves if we are at any point abandoning the unchanging standards of God's Word. For us, living within the culture of our day, it is sometimes hard to see and identify those places where we have shifted. The most obvious shift in our time is probably in attitudes concerning sexuality, which have changed rapidly in recent years amid immense pressure from culture and government.

Recent studies in the United States have highlighted the rapid change in attitudes among those who identify as evangelicals. The Pew Center found that only 26 percent of evangelicals born before 1964 are in favor of same-sex marriage, but 47 percent of those born after 1964 are in favor of it.[4] That is a massive and rapid shift in attitude. It is a very noticeable change on an important hot-button issue. But where else are we shifting? What about attitudes to wealth and generosity, to work and integrity, or to justice and compassion? Where have you and I accommodated ourselves to culture—or simply to our own sinfulness—without noticing?

If the debate over sexuality is one massive moral frontier where culture is pushing hard, another area is the question of the sanctity of life. The Bible teaches us that human beings, whatever their age or health or quality of life, whether in the womb or in palliative care, are made in the image of God and endowed with dignity and worth. Each one is of such worth that God sent His Son for their redemption. Human beings are precious and valuable and worthy of protection at every stage of life. That is what Scripture teaches us. It is a fundamental and unchanging principle of the Word of God and is not up for negotiation. But in Canada, where I live, abortion can be accessed on demand and medically assisted suicide is viewed by many as a fundamental right. And so, inevitably the pressure is on for Christians to shift and adopt a new posture in order to accommodate the culture or the demands of our government. What do we say to these things and how do we respond to the pressure? These are not easy waters to navigate, but the answer is grounded in the simple conviction of the psalmist, "Your word is firmly fixed in the heavens. . . . By your appointment they stand this day" (Ps. 119:89, 91). Our God is immutable and His standards are unchanging.

Human planning is always subject to change. In the church where I serve in Canada's capital city, an unusually large number of folk serve in government. If you spend enough time around government departments, you will soon realize that plans, policies, priorities, and political strategies change all the time. One government works away at a grand plan for health care or defense or transportation and then another government comes in and the priorities are completely reversed, projects are canceled, and something new is dreamt up. It happens all the time. Different leaders have different views, circumstances change, experts revise their advice. But how different it is with God when it comes to His plans and purposes. Nothing ever changes with Him. *God's purposes are unchanging.* And although our world often equates novelty and change with progress, we need to see how very good and wholesome this truth is. The steadfast purpose of the Lord is an anchor for us in a chaotic world, and His unchanging character is the deepest comfort our soul can find.

A number of statements in Paul's epistles give deep insight into God's big-picture plan for the universe. In Ephesians he wrote that God "put all things under his [Jesus'] feet and gave him as head over all things to the church, which is his body, the fullness of him who fills all in all" (Eph. 1:22–23). In the letter to the church in Philippi, he famously made the same point that God's purpose is to exalt Christ and make Him the head over all things:

> Therefore God has highly exalted him and bestowed on
> him the name that is above every name, so that at the name
> of Jesus every knee should bow, in heaven and on earth and
> under the earth, and every tongue confess that Jesus Christ
> is Lord, to the glory of God the Father. (Phil. 2:9–11)

God's grand plan for the universe is to bring all things under the headship of His appointed King, the Lord Jesus Christ, and to cause every knee to bow to Him, either in grace or in judgment. That is the grand divine purpose. It is what God promised all along and it is what He has been doing all along. You and I change our plans all the time—we are fickle creatures—but God is gloriously unlike us in this. "God is not man, that he should lie, or a son of man, that he should change his mind. Has he said, and will he not do it? Or has he spoken, and will he not fulfill it?" (Num. 23:19).

In the 1970s, the Soviet Union built a nuclear reactor in the Armenian community of Metsamor. The plan was to build a model town around this gleaming new plant, but a major earthquake in the 1980s led to safety concerns and the rapid closure of the plant. The grand construction plans for the town were canceled, leaving it half-built. Then an energy crisis in the 1990s prompted the government to reopen part of the plant and so now nine hundred workers live in a half-built town, in an earthquake zone, next to a potentially unsafe nuclear reactor that the government talks of refurbishing one day. It is a fascinating picture of flip-flopping plans and unfulfilled promises.

It strikes me that the story of Metsamor captures so much of the reality of human planning. It is chaotic, ever-changing, and prone to external influences beyond our control. How wonderful, then, that God's purposes and plans are constant; how reassuring that He does not change His mind. For us, that means that we can know for certain what we should be investing ourselves in and what we should be living for. God's purpose in the world is to exalt Jesus as King and to bring all people into a place of submission to Him. That means that our main priority ought to be to submit to Jesus Christ and to live for His honor and glory. If we are working at that each day in the power of the Holy Spirit, then we know we are heading in the right direction. And given that we know God's plan for the universe, the main priority for others around us should be to know, trust, and submit to Jesus Christ. We ought to want them to honor Jesus as King. At the final day, we want them to bow to Him in a position of grace and not judgment.

Living for these things is something we can do with certainty. We need not fear that we might invest our lives in following Jesus as King and proclaiming the risen and ascended Christ only to discover one day that God's plans and priorities have changed.

GOD'S UNCHANGING PROMISES

Human beings are very good at making promises and often very poor at keeping them. That is true of all of us, but I guess our politicians are particularly famous for making outlandish promises that are hard to keep. Former Australian prime minister Bob Hawke famously promised in 1987 that by 1990 no child in Australia would be living in poverty. A grand promise, but of course he could not keep it, and the problem still persists more than thirty-five years later. We make promises—sometimes reckless ones—and are prone to breaking them. Because we know how bad we are at keeping our own promises, we have grown accustomed to doubting the promises of others.

However, the unchanging God is entirely unlike us in this. *God's promises do not change.* "God is not a man, that he should lie, nor a son of man, that he should change his mind," declares the oracle of Balaam. "Has he said, and will he not do it? Or has he spoken, and will he not fulfill it?" (Num. 23:19). The apostle Paul repeated this idea centuries later: "As surely as God is faithful, our word to you has not been Yes and No. For the Son of God, Jesus Christ, whom we proclaimed among you . . . was not Yes and No, but in him it is always Yes," he wrote in his second letter to the Corinthians. "For all the promises of God find their Yes in him" (2 Cor. 1:18–20).

Jesus is the great confirmation that God is a promise-keeping God. He promised a Savior and a deliverer throughout the Old Testament and, in Christ, the Deliverer has come, just as God said He would. Therefore, because those promises have been fulfilled, we know that the unchanging God is always faithful to all He says and to the promises He has made.

This is a very great truth, and it has, if you like, both a negative and positive side. On the negative side, it means that God's warnings of jüdgment are inescapable. We need not look far in Scripture to find that God has given many warnings of judgment. "Be assured, an evil person will not go unpunished" (Prov. 11:21); "For you may be sure of this, that everyone who is sexually immoral or impure, or who is covetous . . . has no inheritance in the kingdom of Christ" (Eph. 5:5). Whenever we hear warnings of judgment and punishment, however, we always hope that the warning will be worse than the reality. *The cop will never give me a ticket for only slightly breaking the limit*, the speeder thinks. *My parents will never actually ground me for that*, the teenager imagines. Or, *the taxman will never penalize me for that small bit of creative accounting*, the businessman hopes. That is the way we often operate. And sometimes it is true. Often the bark is worse than the bite. But we must be careful not to transfer that logic to God. How easily we find ourselves thinking, for instance, that *the God of grace would never condemn me for that sin; the God of love would never actually send anyone to hell.* The eighteenth-century Scottish minister John Dick wrote:

> The Divine immutability . . . has a dark as well as a light side. It insures the execution of His threatenings, as well as the performance of His promises; and destroys the hope which the guilty fondly cherish, that He will be all lenity to His frail and erring creatures, and that they will be much more lightly dealt with than the declarations of His own word would lead us to expect. We oppose to these deceitful and presumptuous speculations the solemn truth, that God is unchanging in veracity and purpose, in faithfulness and justice.[5]

That is, if you will, the negative side of the truth that God's promises are unchanging. It is a truth we all need to hear, especially those who somehow imagine that God would not have it in Him to judge sin and that, ultimately, His grace will extend to everyone in the end. God's promises are unchanging; He will judge sin, and the only place of safety is found in turning from sin and trusting in Christ.

There is also a positive side—a wonderfully hope-filled side—to the truth that God's promises are unchanging. We need only to glance at the Bible to see that it is filled with the most incredible promises to those who belong to the Lord. We could spend a long time looking at these, but let's just read a small handful of them:

> "Be strong and courageous. Do not fear or be in dread of them, for it is the LORD your God who goes with you. He will not leave you or forsake you" (Deut. 31:6)

> "Everyone who calls on the name of the LORD shall be saved" (Joel 2:32)

"All that the Father gives me will come to me, and whoever comes to me I will never cast out" (John 6:37)

"Come to me, all who labor and are heavy laden, and I will give you rest" (Matt. 11:28)

"I am the resurrection and the life. Whoever believes in me, though he die, yet shall he live, and everyone who lives and believes in me shall never die" (John 11:25–26).

We could go on and on. The Word of God is filled with great and precious promises for the people of God. The fact that God never changes tells us that we can trust each and every one of those promises; we can bank on them; we can stake our very lives on them. The God who once made those promises is the very same. He is the God we know and trust today and the God who will deliver us on the final day.

Many of us struggle quite a lot with the question of trust. Perhaps we struggle with it more the longer we live. Children generally start life with a high degree of trust; that is part of the wonder and beauty of childhood. But the hard reality is that the longer we live, the more occasions we have to see our trust violated. Of course, some of us live through terrible traumas—situations of abuse, marital unfaithfulness, fraud in business, betrayal by friends—some, even at the mention of these things, will feel the pain of broken promises afresh. Part of our challenge in walking with the Lord is to learn once more to trust and believe that He will be faithful to what He has said He will do. At the core of our ability to trust God is knowing that He is the unchanging One. It is a vital and glorious truth. Nothing in all the universe has the capacity to bring even the tiniest alteration to the eternal God. He is the same yesterday, today, and forever, and so we know for certain that His word is true and His promises are sure.

four

THE INDEPENDENT GOD

On a prime lakefront location in Toronto sits Ontario Place, an amusement park built in the 1970s and famous for its innovative architecture. The concept was to build a set of large event spaces (or "pods") floating midair above a lagoon. To make this work, the park's engineers put up a single support shaft underneath each massive pod and suspended the frame of the building on wires from the top of that shaft. The visual effect is striking. Visiting the park is like visiting a little futuristic city floating in the air.

Despite the innovation of this, the idea of buildings floating in midair is always going to lead to an imperfect product. You cannot actually make a building float; it has to rest on something, and so the poles underneath each pod are a necessary compromise. In this case, what is true in architecture and engineering is true of everything in the world. Everything depends upon something else. Everything in the world draws its strength, integrity—its very existence—from something else. Everything, that is, except God Himself. He truly is independent of all other things. He needs nothing and depends upon no one and no thing. He is entirely self-sufficient. That is the great truth that the Scriptures celebrate and proclaim. It is the truth that Paul famously proclaimed at the Areopagus in Athens:

> "The God who made the world and everything in it, being Lord of heaven and earth, does not live in temples made by man, nor is he served by human hands, as though he needed anything, since he himself gives to all mankind life and breath and everything." (Acts 17:24–25)

To momentarily repeat Paul, God is not "served by human hands, as though he needed anything." Paul made a point of saying that because he knew that this is a misunderstanding of God that cuts across cultures and religions. Human beings seem instinctively to assume that the Deity *needs something* from us. Christians can fall into that way of thinking too. We can serve and give and pursue holiness all out of a sense that God needs those things from us or is helped in some way by our achievement. But this is a fundamental misconception, as we are going to see.

GOD IS INDEPENDENT IN HIS BEING

The truth that God is not "served by human hands, as though he needed anything" is the point of this chapter, and I would like to begin by looking at God's independence from a few different angles. The first is that *God is not dependent upon anyone for His being*.

Not long ago a tornado touched down not far from our home—mercifully without major incident. Regrettably, the city's system issued the disaster warning once the tornado had already arrived, so that people who were staring at the storm in real time received an alert on their phones telling them that a tornado was passing through. By that point the warning system had the dubious value of stating the blindingly obvious. It is no good getting a storm warning to your phone while you watch your shed being relocated to your neighbor's garden.

With this initial point I feel that I too am stating the blindingly obvious: God made the world but no one made Him. He does not depend upon anyone for His existence. It is a simple fact and a truth with which every Christian must agree. Our God is the uncreated One. It may be a simple truth, but it is at the same time a profoundly important one.

For a start, it is the great truth that sets the true and living God apart from the idols and false gods of other religions. Isaiah draws this out in his prophecy:

> To whom then will you liken God,
>   or what likeness compare with him?
> An idol! A craftsman casts it,
>   and a goldsmith overlays it with gold
>   and casts for it silver chains.
> He who is too impoverished for an offering
>   chooses wood that will not rot;
> he seeks out a skillful craftsman
>   to set up an idol that will not move. . . .
>
> Have you not known? Have you not heard?
> The Lord is the everlasting God,
>   the Creator of the ends of the earth. (Isa. 40:18–20, 28)

Unlike the false gods—in fact, unlike everything else in the universe—God Himself is uncreated, and, as the uncreated One, He is the Creator and the source of all life. John confirmed this at the start of his gospel, "All things were made through him, and without him was not any thing made that was made" (John 1:3).

It is so easy for us to view ourselves more highly than we ought. Our sinful tendency is to place ourselves at the center of the universe and to imagine that the rest of the world and the people around us somehow exist for our purpose and pleasure. But how we need to remember the basic truth that we are the creatures and God is the Creator. He is the great "I Am" who has always existed. He is the First and the Last, the Alpha and the Omega, "who is and who was and who is to come, the Almighty" (Rev. 1:8).

It is an obvious statement, but it is also the fundamental truth with which we need to reckon. Everything flows from this truth. Nonetheless, we manage regularly to forget and overlook it in our self-centered view of the world. The Bible would regularly remind us therefore: the world is not here for our sake; God is not here to serve us or meet our needs; He is the uncreated Creator, and we exist by His power and His will, for His good pleasure. The first aspect of God's independence is the fact that He is dependent upon no one for His being.

The management consultancy business is worth $250 billion a year. Their task is to help others make and execute plans. They help organizations chart the path to success through the choppy seas of change, adversity, and disruption. Fortune 500 companies and governments need that type of support if they are to continue to be successful. But God needs none of it:

> Who has measured the Spirit of the LORD,
> 　　or what man shows him his counsel?
> Whom did he consult,
> 　　and who made him understand?
> Who taught him the path of justice,
> 　　and taught him knowledge,
> 　　and showed him the way of understanding?
> (Isa. 40:13–14)

GOD IS INDEPENDENT IN HIS PLANS AND PURPOSES

In making His plans for the world and the universe, for humanity and salvation, God managed without a single advisor. *God is dependent upon no one for His plans and purposes.* The Bible teaches us that God's plan of redemption stands at the heart of what He is doing in the world and throughout history. And yet it is the universal human instinct to believe that we save ourselves and make ourselves right before God in some way. That is our natural bent, and it is the assumption built in to just about every world religion. But the gospel of Jesus Christ stands apart as so profoundly different.

The great letter to the Ephesians reveals something of this truth. In the opening chapter Paul revealed God's initiative, power, and work in our salvation:

> Blessed be the God and Father of our Lord Jesus Christ, who has blessed us in Christ with every spiritual blessing in the heavenly places, even as he chose us in him before the foundation of the world, that we should be holy and blameless before him. In love he predestined us for adoption to himself as sons through Jesus Christ, according to the purpose of his will, to the praise of his glorious grace, with which he has blessed us in the Beloved. In him we have redemption through his blood, the forgiveness of our trespasses, according to the riches of his grace, which he lavished upon us, in all wisdom and insight. (Eph. 1:3–8)

We could spend multiple chapters dealing with this passage but, for the purposes of this one, what it tells us is this: our salvation is due 100 percent to God. It is His planning, His work in Christ, His initiative, His wider purpose, for the sake of His glory. He does it and we are the glad and privileged recipients of His work.

We add nothing; we contribute nothing; it is all of grace, all for His glory.

GOD IS INDEPENDENT IN HIS BLESSEDNESS

This thought leads neatly to the third point I want to consider in relation to God's independence, which is that *God is not dependent on anyone for His blessedness.* To be blessed is to have all that you need in your life for contentment and fullness. It is a life of happiness. Everyone wants that kind of life, and we naturally search for it in the things of this world. But if the Lord has given us faith, we begin to learn that blessedness is found in Him and through the gospel.

Although we human beings might seek blessedness, God does not need to seek anyone else's blessing because He is fully blessed in eternity. There is nothing lacking in God. There is nothing that He needs to look for elsewhere. The Lord Jesus Himself revealed something of this in John's gospel when He said, "I glorified you on earth, having accomplished the work that you gave me to do. And now, Father, glorify me in your own presence with the glory that I had with you before the world existed" (John 17:4–5). Again, later in the Upper Room Discourse He said, "Father, I desire that they also, whom you have given me, may be with me where I am, to see my glory that you have given me because you loved me before the foundation of the world" (John 17:24).

In other words, before the creation of the world, God was perfectly blessed, enjoying glory and perfect love. The Father, Son, and Holy Spirit lived together in harmonious communion in all eternity, having all that was needed to be whole and complete and entirely blessed. Jonathan Edwards summarized this when he wrote that "God is infinitely happy in the enjoyment of himself, in perfectly beholding and infinitely loving, and rejoicing in, his own essence and perfections."[1] William Perkins declared simply that God is "wholly complete within himself."[2]

When you or I build something or buy something or take on a big project, we always do so out of a sense of lack or desire or need. Maybe it is a need for shelter, so we build a home. Maybe it is a desire for recreation, so we buy a toy. Maybe it is a desire for usefulness, so we take on a project. We can sometimes assume that, because this is always true for us and for those around us, it must be the same for God. We imagine that He made the world because He needed something. Maybe He was lonely, or bored, or (we are more likely to hear or repeat this one) maybe He needed an outlet for His love or an opportunity to display His glory. And so He made humanity for that purpose. Maybe there was some unfulfilled need or lack in God that caused Him to create. We often assume that was the case, at least on some level. But here is the critical truth: God did not need the world. God did not need us. He did not need to create something to plug the gap of some insufficiency in Himself.

In the book of Job, Job's theologically insightful but generally unhelpful friend, Eliphaz, captured this well when he asked:

> "Can a man be profitable to God?
> Surely he who is wise is profitable to himself.
> Is it any pleasure to the Almighty if you are in the right,
> or is it gain to him if you make your ways blameless?"
> (Job 22:2–3)

The answer is clear: none. God does not need anything from you.

It is important in our corporate worship to be careful about the types of songs we sing. Singing, as I understand it, is part of the ministry of the Word and so we ought to only be proclaiming biblical truth in our songs. A popular worship song came out a few years ago and a fellow pastor and I reviewed it to consider its biblical fidelity. At the time the song had an astonishing 300 million views on YouTube and had won a Grammy Award. Much of the song is fine, but there is one line that we tripped over because it suggested that the Lord did not wish to live in heaven if we were not there with Him. The suggestion seemed to be that heaven is just not good enough without the addition of humanity—maybe God is a little lonely in heaven, or like the empty nesters who find the house unbearably quiet. At any rate, we decided not to use the song for fear that it could be theologically confusing, but the sentiment expressed by the song is common enough. In fact, I think the idea is very appealing: God made us and redeemed us because He needed the relationship and company. Three hundred million views on YouTube attest to its appeal. But we must be careful. We are in danger of diminishing and dishonoring God with that line of thought. No, God is happy in Himself. He delights in His Trinitarian relationship of love between the Father, the Son, and the Spirit. He did not need me or you or the world or anyone in it in order to be perfectly happy, blessed, full, and complete.

We live in a very self-centered consumer culture that panders to our every desire. Ours is a world built around self and personal wants and needs. We live in a culture that promotes self-determination and self-expression in every respect. Arguably, our modern parenting methods and education systems often serve to reinforce our natural self-centeredness. That is our culture today. Therefore, to hear the Bible teach that the creation is not about us, that God did not make us because He could not imagine the universe without us, is very offensive to our Western ears. Yet it is the very soul-medicine that we desperately need.

God is dependent upon no one for His being, His plans and purposes, and His blessedness. That is the core of God's independence. The implications of all of this are huge, and I would like to take the remaining pages of this chapter to apply them to three areas of life.

GOD DOES NOT NEED OUR WORSHIP

First, to our *worship*. Properly understood, worship extends beyond what takes place in church on Sunday to the whole of the believer's life and service of God. However, for the moment, I want to think particularly about corporate worship. At the national Science and Technology Museum near our home, there is a room with a big light board with lots of LEDs arranged in dials and bars. In front of the board are three bicycles. Little kids line up to take turns on the bicycles (while parents stand around dutifully on their phones checking to see if anything important has happened on social media in the last three-and-a-half minutes!). The basic idea is that the harder the kids pedal, the more lights they will light up, the farther the dials will go, and the higher the bar will rise. The kids feel a sense of obligation to generate power for the lights, and it becomes a quest and an obsession to make them as bright as possible. As they are panting away—and as *our* kids are reluctant to move on to the next room and the next exhibit—I am tempted to go around the back of the machine to see if I can plug the light display into the power socket at the back so that we can all get on with our lives. All this labor on the part of our children is not needed. There is plenty of power in the mains.

Sometimes I think we come to our corporate worship—and especially our singing—with the view that God's power needs topping up with our efforts. As we block off time on a Sunday morning to listen patiently to God's Word and sing His praises energetically (when we could be in bed or out enjoying the sunshine), we easily assume that God is helped by our contribution, impressed that we have taken the trouble, and grateful that we have spared Him time.

In the Old Testament, biblical worship had at its heart the sacrifice of animals. No one could come before the Lord without a sacrifice. It is different for us now, of course: Jesus has made the perfect sacrifice, and we come to the Father in worship through the Son, our Great High Priest. But casting our minds back to the days of the Old Testament, consider what God says about the worship of His people:

> "Hear, O my people, and I will speak;
>   O Israel, I will testify against you.
>   I am God, your God.
> Not for your sacrifices do I rebuke you;
>   your burnt offerings are continually before me.
> I will not accept a bull from your house
>   or goats from your folds.
> For every beast of the forest is mine,
>   the cattle on a thousand hills.
> I know all the birds of the hills,
>   and all that moves in the field is mine.
>
> "If I were hungry, I would not tell you,
>   for the world and its fullness are mine.
> Do I eat the flesh of bulls
>   or drink the blood of goats?
> Offer to God a sacrifice of thanksgiving,
>   and perform your vows to the Most High,
> and call upon me in the day of trouble;
>   I will deliver you, and you shall glorify me." (Ps. 50:7–15)

Does God need something from us? Is there anything He lacks that by our worship we can fulfill? Of course not. In fact, it is the other way around. As we approach the Lord to worship Him, we do not come primarily to give; we actually come to receive. He invited us to "call upon me in the day of trouble; I will deliver you, and you shall glorify me" (v. 15). This is exactly the point that Paul drove home in Acts 17, as I outlined earlier in the chapter.

Theologian John Frame put the matter simply when he wrote, "Biblical worship, unlike much pagan worship, is not intended to meet the needs of its God . . . in worship we offer our thanks for the fact that God has met our needs."[3] We worship with empty hands—with nothing to offer—and we call upon God for His gracious help, to thank Him for what He has done in Christ. With our divided hearts and stuttering lips, we express something of our feeble understanding of who He is in all His majesty, glory, and goodness. As we do that, we receive the encouragement of His work and the blessing of His help. We come to worship as recipients and respondents, but not as those who have something needful to give the God who is perfectly happy, full, and blessed in and of Himself.

Much of this probably runs contrary to many of our instincts and assumptions about worship, but if we grasp this truth, it will have a transformative effect on our corporate worship. If we understand it, we will lose our swagger and sense of triumphalism and we will refuse to allow anyone other than the Lord to have the glory. We will come in a spirit of reverence and awe, of humility and emptiness, of joy and gratitude. That is worship.

GOD DOES NOT NEED OUR GIVING

Still, the implications of God's independence go further. They touch our *giving* as well. It is interesting to consider why we give to the work of the gospel. Have you ever paused to consider why God has set things up in this way—that His work in reaching the nations with the good news of Jesus should happen through the gifts of His people? If we have learned anything about God's independence, we know He is not reliant upon us for anything, and this must, of course, include our giving. After all, the whole world is His. We have already considered the words of the psalmist, "I will not accept a bull from your house or goats from your folds. For every beast of the forest is mine, the cattle on a thousand hills" (Ps. 50:9–10). Psalm 24 expresses the same thought: "The earth is the Lord's and the fullness thereof, the world and those who dwell therein, for he has founded it upon the seas and established it upon the rivers" (Ps. 24:1–2). We certainly do not give to the Lord and His work because He needs our money. There must, therefore, be something else going on, some other dynamic at play.

We are given a helpful insight into this dynamic in a wonderful passage in 1 Chronicles 29. The people of Israel have just given very generously to the work of building the temple, and King David is moved to cry out in praise to the Lord:

> David blessed the Lord in the presence of all the assembly. And David said: "Blessed are you, O Lord, the God of Israel our father, forever and ever. Yours, O Lord, is the greatness and the power and the glory and the victory and the majesty, for all that is in the heavens and in the earth is yours. Yours is the kingdom, O Lord, and you are exalted as head above all. Both riches and honor come from you, and you rule over all. In your hand are power and might, and in your hand it is to make great and to give strength to all. And now we thank you, our God, and praise your glorious name.
>
> "But who am I, and what is my people, that we should be able thus to offer willingly? For all things come from you, and of your own have we given you. For we are strangers

before you and sojourners, as all our fathers were. Our days on the earth are like a shadow, and there is no abiding. O LORD our God, all this abundance that we have provided for building you a house for your holy name comes from your hand and is all your own." (vv. 10–16)

If you believe that you are giving to the Lord because He needs it, your giving will only go so far. If any of us give in that way, we will only balance the Lord's imagined needs with what we sense are our own needs (and maybe the desire for our next vacation or new car will win out). Similarly, if you give money that you believe belongs to you, you will give reluctantly, and when you do give, you will always be tempted to self-congratulate. But David modeled for us a different understanding and a different outlook. Everything in the world belongs to the Lord. All our assets are His. What a privilege it is, therefore, to be able to participate in the Lord's work by giving back to Him what is already His. He has enabled us to give so that we might have an opportunity to declare and display something of His majesty and His worth.

Our giving, then, reflects the vision and comprehension we have of God Himself. Rather than being about us, it is about understanding who He is, the glorious Creator and all-sufficient One. The Lord, wonderfully, gives us freedom in this, but our challenge is to pray over the question: What does our giving reveal of our understanding of God? Does our giving reflect the fact that He is worthy of all glory and honor? God does not need our money; but what we do with our money reveals a great deal of what we think of Him.

A lovely old hymn written by William Walsham How is not sung very often anymore, but it captures so well the truth we have been considering:

We give thee but thine own,
whate'er the gift may be;
all that we have is thine alone,
a trust, O Lord, from thee.

May we thy bounties thus
as stewards true receive
and gladly, as thou blessest us,
to thee our first fruits give.[4]

GOD DOES NOT NEED OUR SERVICE

The final point I want to make in relation to God's independence has to do with our *service*. A. W. Tozer wrote:

> Probably the hardest thought of all for our natural egotism to entertain is that God does not need our help. We commonly represent Him as a busy, eager, somewhat frustrated Father hurrying about seeking help to carry out His benevolent plan to bring peace and salvation to the world. . . . I fear that thousands of younger persons enter Christian service from no higher motive than to help deliver God from the embarrassing situation His love has gotten Him into and His limited abilities seem unable to get Him out of.[5]

As believers, we have the opportunity to participate in what God is doing in the world. This is an immense privilege. When so many in our world are struggling to find meaning in what appears to them to be a meaningless existence, we have the opportunity to take part in God's great plan to exalt His Son and to bring all things under the headship of Jesus. It is a tremendous privilege, but, as with our giving, we do not serve because God needs us and we ought not to expect praise and adulation for serving the One who created us and then gave His Son to redeem us.

In a rather hard-hitting passage in Luke's gospel, Jesus made this point quite bluntly and in a way that runs the risk of wounding our pride:

> "Will any one of you who has a servant plowing or keeping sheep say to him when he has come in from the field, 'Come at once and recline at table'? Will he not rather say to him, 'Prepare supper for me, and dress properly, and serve me while I eat and drink, and afterward you will eat and drink'? Does he thank the servant because he did what was commanded? So you also, when you have done all that you were commanded, say, 'We are unworthy servants; we have only done what was our duty.'" (Luke 17:7–10)

It is good to serve in the work of the gospel; it is right and necessary to do so if we are followers of Christ. And, of course, it is nice to thank and encourage one another when we are helped or blessed by the ministry and service of others. But, as we serve, let us never imagine that we are doing God a favor or helping Him out of a tough spot. Let us serve because it is a privilege. Let us serve because He is worthy. Let us rejoice in the opportunity and humbly offer ourselves to Him.

It is never comfortable to be put in our place, but as we think about the independence of God—the sheer self-sufficiency of the almighty and glorious God—we are gently brought down to size.

We easily set ourselves at the center of our own universe. That is actually the very nature of sin. Even as believers, we tend to make things about ourselves all too readily. But the truth is that God has no need of us, and the story of the universe is not all about us. In His grace and mercy and love, God has not only created us and redeemed us, but He involves us in His work. Our response to all these things must be that of the apostle Paul as he contemplated the sheer wisdom and power of God:

> Oh, the depth of the riches and wisdom and knowledge of God! How unsearchable are his judgments and how inscrutable his ways!
>
> > "For who has known the mind of the Lord,
> > > or who has been his counselor?"
> > "Or who has given a gift to him
> > > that he might be repaid?"
>
> For from him and through him and to him are all things. To him be glory forever. (Rom. 11:33–36)

five

THE INCOMPREHENSIBLE GOD

According to legend, Augustine of Hippo was one day walking along the beach when he came upon a small boy scooping up water with a shell. The two of them struck up a conversation and Augustine asked the boy what he was doing; he replied that he was emptying the sea. Augustine tried to tell him that you cannot do that—that it was a futile exercise. Eventually Augustine went on his way and, as he did, he began to reflect on the exchange. If that little boy could not scoop up the sea with his little shell, how much less could he, a human thinker, understand the infinite God.[1]

The theme of this chapter is the incomprehensibility of God. That is, the truth that God is not fully knowable in all that He is. To say that God is incomprehensible is not to say that we cannot know God in any sense. We can know God and, as believers, we *do* know God. But Christians have long used the language of incomprehensibility to express the truth that it is impossible for us, as finite creatures, to fully grasp the infinite God. We cannot know God as He knows Himself. It is more than we could expect and manage. It is also more than God has given us to know.

It is a serious error to imagine that we can wrap our finite minds around all God's being and all His doing. In Scripture, that error is perhaps most dramatically illustrated by Job's profoundly unhelpful friends who met him and sought to counsel him in his suffering. The lengthy narrative of Job's painful interactions with these friends is a powerful cautionary tale of what can go wrong when any mere mortal presumes to speak as though he or she fully comprehends God. Job's friends had a rather mechanistic view of God; if a person is suffering, God has inflicted that suffering on him in response to a particular sin. This simplistic (and inaccurate) view of God is shown to be dangerous because it adds to Job's already horrific suffering. This, then, is a case in point: theology matters, and a humble acceptance of and belief in the incomprehensibility of God is vitally important. It is dangerous and often damaging to presume to speak more than we know about God's will and His ways. It is sobering to hear God's response to these presumptuous friends, "My anger burns against you and against your two friends, for you have not spoken of me what is right, as my servant Job has" (Job 42:7). Evidently God takes it very seriously when His creatures presume to speak for Him and about Him in ways that go beyond their knowledge.

WE DO NOT KNOW EVERYTHING ABOUT GOD

Some years ago A. W. Tozer expressed his concern that Christians were reducing the infinite God down to a more convenient size and imagining that they could fully comprehend Him. "Left to ourselves we tend immediately to reduce God to manageable terms," he wrote, before continuing:

> We want to get Him where we can use Him, or at least know where He is when we need Him. We want a God we can in some measure control. We need the feeling of security that comes from knowing what God is like, and what He is like is, of course, a composite of all the religious pictures we have seen, all the best people we have known or heard about, and all the sublime ideas we have entertained. If all this sounds strange to modern ears, it is only because we have for a full half-century taken God for granted. The glory of God has not been revealed to this generation of men. The God of contemporary Christianity is only slightly superior to the gods of Greece and Rome if indeed He is not actually inferior to them in that He is weak and helpless while they at least had power.[2]

Tozer, I think, hit the nail right on the head. The danger he saw in his day, six decades ago, remains in our day. Our great need is to see that the God of eternity, the God of creation, our Lord and Redeemer, our Judge and King, is bigger and greater than our finite minds could ever conceive. This leads us into the first point, which is the truth that *God has not revealed Himself exhaustively* to us.

As I have already mentioned, in the church in which I serve there are a number of people who work in the Canadian federal government. They tell me that there are different levels of security clearance given for particular roles. The Canadian Security Intelligence Service manages the security clearance program, under which, I understand, there are four levels of clearance, topping out at the "enhanced top secret level." If you operate within the misty world of security or defense, you know that, depending on your clearance level, there are certain things that have been made known to you—certain types of information to which you have been given access—as well as certain things that have not been made known to you. That is just the way it is. Everyone understands that there are good reasons for giving and withholding information.

When it comes to our knowledge of God, I think we tend to assume that we have the right to know everything that can be known about Him. However, as we look closely at Scripture, we find that this is simply not the case. God's Word makes it clear that there are aspects of divine knowledge that are not given to us to know.

When Moses delivered a message from the Lord to the people of Israel at Moab, he declared that "the secret things belong to the LORD our God, but the things that are revealed belong to us and to our children forever, that we may do all the words of this law" (Deut. 29:29). This is a fascinating statement. It tells us that there are essentially two categories of knowledge. On the one hand, the secret things belong only to God; on the other hand, God, in his wisdom and kindness, has chosen to make the revealed things known to us. There are levels of clearance when it comes to divine knowledge, if you like, and the top-level clearance belongs only to God Himself. Why this is the case, we do not fully know, but unquestionably an element of this is for our own protection. We can see or comprehend only so much of God in His glory and power without being entirely overwhelmed and even destroyed.

This truth is powerfully illustrated in a striking incident in the Exodus narrative when Moses asked the Lord if he could see Him:

> Moses said to the LORD, "See, you say to me, 'Bring up this people,' but you have not let me know whom you will send with me. Yet you have said, 'I know you by name, and you have also found favor in my sight.' Now therefore, if I have

found favor in your sight, please show me now your ways, that I may know you in order to find favor in your sight. Consider too that this nation is your people." And he said, "My presence will go with you, and I will give you rest." And he said to him, "If your presence will not go with me, do not bring us up from here. For how shall it be known that I have found favor in your sight, I and your people? Is it not in your going with us, so that we are distinct, I and your people, from every other people on the face of the earth?"

And the LORD said to Moses, "This very thing that you have spoken I will do, for you have found favor in my sight, and I know you by name." Moses said, "Please show me your glory." And he said, "I will make all my goodness pass before you and will proclaim before you my name 'The LORD.' And I will be gracious to whom I will be gracious, and will show mercy on whom I will show mercy. But," he said, "you cannot see my face, for man shall not see me and live." And the LORD said, "Behold, there is a place by me where you shall stand on the rock, and while my glory passes by I will put you in a cleft of the rock, and I will cover you with my hand until I have passed by. Then I will take away my hand, and you shall see my back, but my face shall not be seen." (Ex. 33:12–23)

Moses wanted to know God—His name and His ways—and God promised to be with Moses and go with His people and proclaim His name in their presence. Then Moses said he wanted to see God, and God said: I will put you in the cleft of the rock, cover you with My hand as I pass by, and when I remove My hand, you will see My back. That is as far as it can possibly go. You cannot see My face. The sight of God as He truly is, in all His glory and majesty, is more than a human being can manage or absorb. We cannot see or encounter the very essence of God.

The Scottish theologian Thomas Boston wrote that God, in His infinite being, "lies hid in rays of such bright and radiant glory, as must for ever dazzle the eyes of those who attempt to look into it."[3] It is like trying to look at the sun. It is destructive for our eyes and too much for us to manage.[4] Of course, that should not surprise us. If God is truly God, and if we truly are His creatures, we should expect to be limited in our ability to comprehend Him. Even if God chose to tell us everything there was to know about Him, we could never process it nor fully comprehend it. Scripture after Scripture reminds us that the God of heaven is bigger and more glorious, more wonderful, and more majestic than we can ever fully know:

> "[God] does great things and unsearchable,
> marvelous things without number." (Job 5:9)

> "Can you find out the deep things of God?
> Can you find out the limit of the Almighty?
> It is higher than heaven—what can you do?
> Deeper than Sheol—what can you know?
> Its measure is longer than the earth
> and broader than the sea." (Job 11:7–9)

> Great is the Lord, and greatly to be praised,
> and his greatness is unsearchable. (Ps. 145:3)

> Have you not known? Have you not heard?
> The Lord is the everlasting God,
> the Creator of the ends of the earth.
> He does not faint or grow weary;
> his understanding is unsearchable. (Isa. 40:28)

"For my thoughts are not your thoughts,
  neither are your ways my ways, declares the LORD.
For as the heavens are higher than the earth,
  so are my ways higher than your ways
  and my thoughts than your thoughts." (Isa. 55:8–9)

No one can fathom the greatness or the mysteries of God. His thoughts and His ways are higher than ours. He has not made Himself fully known to us, but has kept some things secret. Even what He has revealed is more than we can fully process. As Christian theologians have affirmed through the centuries, *the finite cannot contain the infinite.*

Our limitless God is incomprehensible to us limited and finite creatures. We will never know Him as He knows Himself. This might seem disappointing. But I want to suggest that this is actually good news. In our age, when we have the world's information at our fingertips, it is frustrating for us not to know something. It sounds like bad news to our ears that God has not revealed Himself exhaustively to us and remains incomprehensible. But this truth is a comfort for us because, at the end of the day, we actually want to know—*and need to know*—that there are those whose knowledge and ability goes beyond our own. Imagine you are heading into a major medical procedure. You do not ever want to reach a point where you feel you know as much as the surgeon knows. What you want and need to know before you lie on the table and close your eyes is that the surgeon's knowledge and ability go far beyond yours. That is what really matters to you. If you and I felt we could put God in a box and have Him all figured out, we would find ourselves in a vulnerable and frightening situation. But praise God that His knowledge and being go far beyond anything we could ever comprehend.

WE DO KNOW WHAT GOD
HAS REVEALED ABOUT HIMSELF

If God has not revealed Himself exhaustively, then the second thing to consider is that *God has revealed Himself truly*. Although our knowledge of God is limited, in His grace and mercy, He has gone out of His way to reveal Himself to us. In fact, if God had not chosen to reveal Himself as He has, we would be entirely in the dark about Him. Psalm 19 tells us that He has done this, in part, through the creation that we see around us:

> The heavens declare the glory of God,
>> and the sky above proclaims his handiwork.
> Day to day pours out speech,
>> and night to night reveals knowledge.
> There is no speech, nor are there words,
>> whose voice is not heard.
> Their voice goes out through all the earth,
>> and their words to the end of the world. (Ps. 19:1–4)

As I was working on this chapter, I noticed a blossom on the tree outside the window of my study. And, in observing it, I was struck by the generosity, artistry, and kindness of God in making a world that is as beautiful and bountiful as this. Simply observing the hand of God in creation in this way gives us a responsibility to respond to Him with gratitude and praise. Paul picked up the essential truth of Psalm 19 in his letter to the Romans when he drew out the following basic but very sobering implication:

> For the wrath of God is revealed from heaven against all ungodliness and unrighteousness of men, who by their unrighteousness suppress the truth. For what can be known about God is plain to them, because God has shown it

to them. For his invisible attributes, namely, his eternal power and divine nature, have been clearly perceived, ever since the creation of the world, in the things that have been made. So they are without excuse. For although they knew God, they did not honor him as God or give thanks to him, but they became futile in their thinking, and their foolish hearts were darkened. (Rom. 1:18–21)

We do not know everything about God by looking at the trees in bloom, or by gazing on the mountains and the seas, or by looking at the animals in all their diversity, or by examining the intricacy and complexity of the human mind, but we do know enough about Him from any one of those things to bow down and worship. In fact, Paul says that to fail to do so is culpable before God.

Of course, God has done more than simply leave His creative imprint on the world. He has actually spoken to us. In the Old Testament, He gave His law and sent prophets to speak His word. At the same time, His Old Testament word pointed forward to a deliverer who would come and address the problem of sin, of human guilt and rebellion. Therefore, when Jesus came on the scene in the New Testament, John referred to Him as the Word made flesh (John 1:14). He Himself is the fulfillment of the promises of God. Through the Scriptures, and in the person of Jesus Christ, we have the comprehensive Word of God—the full revelation. Not that God has told us *everything*, but He has told us all that we need to know in order to honor Him obediently as Creator.

Remember, again, what God said in Deuteronomy, "The secret things belong to the LORD our God, but the things that are revealed belong to us and to our children forever, that we may do all the words of this law" (Deut. 29:29). What God has told us, He has told us to enable us to respond to Him in obedience and faith. That is His purpose, and His revealed Word is all that we need.

I often think back to the hymn:

> How firm a foundation, ye saints of the Lord,
> is laid for your faith in His excellent Word!
> What more can he say than you to you God hath said,
> to you who for refuge to Jesus have fled?[5]

"What more can he say?" There is a fullness to His revelation to us. We could not cope with His complete self-revelation. Nonetheless, in the Word of God we have His true, rich, and sufficient revelation of Himself.

WE CAN KNOW GOD HIMSELF

What, then, are we to make of these things? Let me suggest three ways in which we need to respond practically to the self-revelation of this gloriously incomprehensible God. First, *we need to humbly accept what we do not know*. We all find it annoying when we do not know something. It starts in childhood. You only have to see another child whisper in the ear of a friend in the schoolyard to know the rising indignation that comes when you feel out of the loop. There is a sense of urgency to know and a sense of injustice that you have been excluded. We all feel as though we should be fully informed. When it comes to knowing and understanding God, it can drive us to distraction if we feel that we have a question that is unanswered or, worse still, unanswerable.

For people who are exploring the Christian faith, this can be a real obstacle. They may have a question about God and feel there are limitations to the answers they are getting. Or, as believers, we encounter a situation where two truths about God do not seem to sit well together and we cannot reconcile them perfectly. These things can trouble us. The danger will always be that we end up in a position of frustration or doubt and that we give up in despair. But I would like to suggest that this dynamic is actually just what we should expect. We should expect to hit some dead-end roads when we consider the deep things of God. We need to learn to accept the fact that we are the creatures and not the Creator, that we do not have a right answer to every question, and that there is a necessary place for faith—for trusting the God whom we do not fully understand. Ultimately, if we could find every answer to our questions about God, and understand every answer we received, then the God we worshiped would be a small god, unworthy of our praise and adoration.

If we need to humbly accept what we do not know, then *we also need to be responsive to what we do know.* When we come to see that there are questions about God for which we do not have an answer, it is easy for us to become fixated on those gaps in our knowledge and understanding, but the truth is that God has told us more in His Word than we will ever fully grasp. "What more can he say, than to you he hath said?" More than one lifetime of truth is contained within the Bible, and I think all of us who spend time digging into the Word only find that, the further we go, the more we have to learn. Therefore, we need to be careful not to fixate on what is unknown—in other words, what God has chosen not to reveal—and rather give ourselves to responding to what He has said.

I am fascinated by aircraft and take some interest in them. Whenever I fly I am keen to know a little about the plane in which I am traveling. I always find myself looking through the publications in the seat pocket to see if there is anything of interest about the aircraft. Inevitably, there never really is. The in-flight magazine may have some general information about the airline's fleet, which will only ever tell you very basic facts about the plane. Then, of course, there is the safety card, which is never satisfying either. Yet the safety card is actually a vitally important document. The information that it gives me about the plane is crucial. It tells me how the plane will keep me safe in a dangerous situation and how to benefit from the safety that the plane can provide. It tells me what to do and what not to do on the plane, but it will not tell me other things that I would like to know. It will not tell me the history of the plane's design, nor where the components were made and assembled, nor about the navigation systems or engine specifications. But it tells me what I actually need to know if I am going to travel safely on the plane.

The Bible is not here to satisfy all my curiosity about God. It does not exist to answer any and every question I may have. It *is* here, however, to tell me that I am a sinner and that God sent His Son to rescue me. It tells me that I must respond to Him in repentance and faith. It tells me that God requires my obedience. The constant danger for us is that we will set aside the safety card, if you like, because it does not scratch the itch of our curiosity. We will close our minds and our hearts to God's revelation of Himself in the Scriptures because we have questions that are not yet answered. In doing that, we will fail to hear the message of salvation that God's Word brings; we will fail to heed the call to repent and believe; we will fail to respond to the requirement to obey.

The Bible does not resolve every question for us. We do not know God as He knows Himself and we do not have insight into every aspect of His being. But while God may not have given us insight or capacity to know Him exhaustively, He has invited us to know Him *truly*. He has come to us in the person of His Son to reveal Himself to us, and He has placed His call on our lives.

When Jesus appeared on the scene in Galilee, His call to the people was simple, "Repent and believe in the gospel" (Mark 1:15). Turn from your sin and believe that I have come to save you from the consequences and destruction of sin. Those who first responded in repentance and faith did not examine the origin of God or the mechanics of Christ's incarnation, or the validity of Jesus' claims against those of other religions, or sit down and debate with Him the origin of evil. All those discussions are valid, and the Christian faith is intellectually coherent and bears close examination. Yet sometimes the debate and the questioning actually become the excuse not to respond.

God's revelation to us is not given to satisfy every question we have. His revelation is given to call us to faith and then to a life of obedience. When we are struggling with God's work we need to ask the question: Is my problem intellectual at its core or is my problem that I do not like what the Word of God says? That is the point of Deuteronomy 29:29. The secret things belong to God. The revealed things belong to His people that "we may do all the words of this law."

God has given His revelation for the sake of obedience. Obedience is not complicated, but it is very hard: "What does the LORD require of you but to do justice, and to love kindness, and to walk humbly with your God?" (Mic. 6:8). These are hard things to do, but they are not complicated to understand. It is easy for us to use questions and doubts and intellectual problems to skirt obedience. They can be great smokescreens. It is quite possible that some who are reading this book are holding off submitting their whole heart and life to Jesus Christ ostensibly because of some intellectual question or problem, but actually, in all honesty and sincerity, the core issue is a nervousness of what it will look like, what it will cost, to submit to Jesus as Lord.

Perhaps your situation is different. You are a believer, but you sense that you are allowing yourself to drift away from the Lord. You are allowing your heart to grow cool toward Him, and what you are saying to yourself or others is that you have encountered some major intellectual barrier. There is some aspect of God's

Word that you do not understand or cannot logically reconcile. If you are being honest with yourself, that questioning is now becoming an excuse for disobedience, for drifting and wandering. Maybe, if you are being *really* honest with yourself, the problem is that you just do not like what God has quite clearly said. If that is the case, let me urge you to be careful. We may have honest and sincere questions, and it is right and legitimate to bring those to God's Word and work through them as best as we can, but we need to take care never to allow our questioning to become a cover for disobedience and an excuse to sidestep the Word of God.

We must humbly accept what we do not know, we must be responsive to what we do know, and finally, *we must be hungry to know more.* In the Psalms David wrote, "How precious to me are your thoughts, O God! How vast is the sum of them! If I would count them, they are more than the sand" (Ps. 139:17–18). For David, the knowledge that the thoughts of God are vast in sum—outnumbering the grains of sand by the sea—makes those thoughts more precious and more wonderful to him. When it comes to knowing God, there is always more to know and, in fact, the more we know of him, the more we realize how little we know and the more we hunger to grow in our knowledge.

Of course, something of this is natural when it comes to any relationship. As we get to know someone—in friendship, in family, in marriage—however long we have known a person, we always have more to discover. Those who are married know this especially well: you never reach a point in marriage (even after thirty or forty years!) when you stop learning more about the other person. That is part of the joy and wonder of it. God has revealed more of Himself to us in His Word than we will ever comprehend in this lifetime. There is always more of Him to know and to experience. If we are believers, we long to know Him better.

I was recently reading through Jeremiah and I came across this wonderful exhortation:

> Thus says the LORD: "Let not the wise man boast in his wisdom, let not the mighty man boast in his might, let not the rich man boast in his riches, but let him who boasts boast in this, that he understands and knows me." (Jer. 9:23–24)

Knowing the Lord is at the core of who we are and what we do as God's people. It is the essence of life. Remember that Jesus says, "And this is eternal life, that they know you, the only true God, and Jesus Christ whom you have sent" (John 17:3). Eternal life is knowing God. He is the incomprehensible one. There are depths to Him that we will never plumb, there are heights that we will never reach, but there is an eternity's worth of growing in knowledge of Him.

I wonder if you and I are hungry to know Him more. I wonder if that is what we boast in—knowing the Lord as He has made Himself known. I wonder if this majestic and glorious God is our delight and if thinking of Him consumes our mental energy, fills our heart, and drives us to His Word.

Where we reach the limits of our understanding, we need to learn to move from inquiry and contemplation to praise and adoration. The Puritan Thomas Watson wrote this:

> We can no more search out [God's] infinite perfections, than a man upon the top of the highest mountain can reach the firmament, or take a star in his hand. Oh, have God-admiring thoughts! Adore where you cannot fathom. . . . In heaven we shall see God clearly, but not fully, for he is infinite; he will communicate himself to us, according to the bigness of our vessel, but not the immenseness of his nature. Adore then where you cannot fathom.[6]

Our great God is incomprehensible. If we belong to Him, our heart's desire is to know Him better through His Word, but where we reach the end of knowledge and understanding—what good advice that is—let us learn to adore Him all the more.

six

THE ALL-KNOWING, ALL-WISE GOD

A rtificial intelligence has come a long way in recent years. For many people it is hard to imagine life without the latest mobile phone or personal device. Of course, the more you interact with these systems, the more impressive they seem. It can even feel as though their capacity is endless and their knowledge limitless. I was driving along in the car a little while ago and wanted to put a call in to my mother. In doing so I thought it would be a good opportunity to test out my phone's capability, and so I said to my phone, "Hey Siri, call my mother." Anticipating that the call would begin right away, I was surprised that Siri instead took it upon herself to answer with something of an impertinent tone, "I'm sorry, I don't know who your mother is. In fact, I don't know who you are."

The world holds a great deal of knowledge—more, even, than the greatest supercomputers will ever know—but the knowledge compiled by humanity, with all our clever systems, is but a drop in the bucket of all that there is to know. No library, no server, no system of artificial intelligence can claim to hold even a fraction of all that is knowable. But the Scriptures claim without embarrassment that our Creator God, the eternal One, truly knows and understands all things. The psalmist declared, "Great is our Lord, and abundant in power; his understanding is beyond measure" (Ps. 147:5). The apostle John put the matter simply in his first epistle, telling us that God "knows everything" (1 John 3:20).

Being eternal and unchanging, the God who knows all things never grows in His knowledge, He is never surprised by anything, and His degree of insight and understanding never develops. In His eternity He knows everything there is to know, including all that has ever happened, is now happening, and will ever happen. In fact, He knows all things that *could* happen but do not actually happen. To make it all the more remarkable, He knows all this fully and at once. Add to this the fact that He knows all that is going on in every place on earth and that there is no activity or event of which He is unaware.

Solomon told us, "The eyes of the LORD are in every place, keeping watch on the evil and the good" (Prov. 15:3). In his wonderful declaration of praise, Daniel declared that "to [God] belong wisdom and might. He changes times and seasons; he removes kings and sets up kings; he gives wisdom to the wise and knowledge to those who have understanding; he reveals deep and hidden things; he knows what is in the darkness" (Dan. 2:20b–22). God sees all things, He knows all things, and in His wisdom He knows how to use that knowledge to the very best purpose and end. God is both all-knowing and all-wise; that is what Daniel is saying, and it is the theme and subject of this sixth chapter.

As with every aspect of God's character, this truth is not merely theoretical; it is deeply practical, and failing to grasp and believe it leaves us spiritually vulnerable. Rightly understood, it should shape our walk with Jesus in a profound way. As we are going to see, knowing and believing that God is all-knowing and all-wise is a powerful guard against sin and a wonderful encouragement toward faith. So, let us look closely at this truth together.

GOD HAS PERFECT KNOWLEDGE OF US

We begin with the knowledge of God and the truth that *God has perfect knowledge of us*. Now if people believe in God at all, my guess would be that most assume that He sees what is taking place in the world. But people tend to imagine that His knowledge of individuals and events is a kind of bird's-eye view, an overview from above, like the view that an operator of a security camera might have of the activities in a large public building, peering at grainy and distant images of people scurrying beneath. But the reality is far different. The Bible tells us that God sees into the heart of each person and knows all that there is to know.

As our Creator He knows us intimately. He knows how we were made and He knows our weaknesses and frailties, "As a father shows compassion to his children, so the LORD shows compassion to those who fear him. For he knows our frame" (Ps. 103:13–14a). More than that, he knows what is going on inside our hearts and minds:

> O LORD, you have searched me and known me!
> You know when I sit down and when I rise up;
>   you discern my thoughts from afar.
> You search out my path and my lying down
>   and are acquainted with all my ways.
> Even before a word is on my tongue,
>   behold, O LORD, you know it altogether. (Ps. 139:1–4)

Because the Lord has such intimate knowledge of us, He can say of His covenant people, "Before they call I will answer; while they are yet speaking I will hear" (Isa. 65:24).

Parents of small children often know what their children will ask for before they have thought of it themselves. In the middle of the night, almost before a child wakes, a parent might be awake, sensing the need, anticipating what will come next. Before we even cry out to our heavenly Father, He knows our need and He knows what is on our heart. Before we gather our thoughts sufficiently even to articulate the prayer—or the cry—of our heart, He knows all about it. In short, He knows us completely and He knows us better than we know ourselves.

Perhaps you have never thought much about that, but it is one of the most comforting truths we can ever consider. How amazing to think how thoroughly God knows us. He understands our bodies and how they function. This means that if you are in the midst of a medical investigation and there is something wrong that no one can diagnose, God knows what it is. He knit you together, and He sees better than any X-ray or scan what is going on. He loves you and cares for you, and He has power to heal you if that is His will; and, if not, He has power to sustain you, come what may.

He knows our quiet sorrows and secret griefs and the things that are hard to share with others. He knows and understands; He is listening and is ready to help and to work out His good purposes. When we are in difficulty, it is easy to imagine that God has overlooked us or forgotten us. But none of His children escapes His view and no one is beyond His care and concern. Whatever is going on, here is the believer's great comfort: our loving, powerful, and good Father in heaven knows all about it. Nothing has escaped His notice.

This is a wonderfully comforting truth for the child of God, but it is also a searching truth that brings a deep challenge. The writer to the Hebrews tell us that "no creature is hidden from his sight, but all are naked and exposed to the eyes of him to whom we must give account" (Heb. 4:13). The God who sees and hears the cry of our hearts also sees the secrets of our hearts—the things we would prefer no one knew about. So the psalmist can say, "If we had forgotten the name of our God or spread out our hands to a foreign god, would not God discover this? For he knows the secrets of the heart" (Ps. 44:20–21), or again, "He who teaches man knowledge—the LORD—knows the thoughts of man, that they are but a breath" (Ps. 94:10b–11), or again, "You have set our iniquities before you, our secret sins in the light of your presence" (Ps. 90:8). The truth that these verses reveal is that the God who sees our heart better than we do also sees our sin with total clarity.

Despite the foolishness of doing so, it is easy to imagine that we can hide from God. When small children do something they do not want to own up to, their instinct is often to cover their eyes. If I cannot see Mummy or Daddy (so the logic goes), then Mummy or Daddy cannot see me. But it is just like Adam and Eve hiding in the Garden of Eden imagining that God will not see them and find out their sin. It is like Cain hoping that the Lord might not realize that he has murdered his brother Abel. But, of course, God saw it all. "What have you done?" he said to Cain. "The voice of your brother's blood is crying to me from the ground" (Gen. 4:10). Nothing can be hidden from the Lord. We may fool others, concealing sin for a long time. Even great crimes can go unsolved and unpunished in this life. But the Lord sees and the Lord knows.

Perhaps the most dramatic and sobering story of this kind in all Scripture is found in the book in Joshua. The people of Israel had just taken the city of Jericho by the Lord's gracious help. As they went into the city the Lord gave the solemn instruction that the spoil from the city should be kept aside and devoted to Him. Nonetheless, we read that "the people of Israel broke faith in regard to the devoted things, for Achan the son of Carmi, son of Zabdi, son of Zerah, of the tribe of Judah, took some of the devoted things. And the anger of the LORD burned against the people of Israel" (Josh. 7:1). Achan thought he had been clever. He thought he had been shrewd and had covered his tracks by hiding the treasure in his tent. But the Lord saw, and in the next battle Israel was routed and the heart of the people melted. The Lord made it clear to Joshua: you have got to deal with this issue before you will know My blessing again; you have got to get the people to come forward tribe by tribe, clan by clan, family by family, until the culprit is identified. Through this procedure, Achan was quickly singled out, and the harrowing tale unfolds:

> Then Joshua said to Achan, "My son, give glory to the LORD God of Israel and give praise to him. And tell me now what you have done; do not hide it from me." And Achan answered Joshua, "Truly I have sinned against the LORD God of Israel, and this is what I did: when I saw among the spoil a beautiful cloak from Shinar, and 200 shekels of silver, and a bar of gold weighing 50 shekels, then I coveted them and took them. And see, they are hidden in the earth inside my tent, with the silver underneath."
>
> So Joshua sent messengers, and they ran to the tent; and behold, it was hidden in his tent with the silver underneath. And they took them out of the tent and brought them to Joshua and to all the people of Israel. And they laid them down before the LORD. And Joshua and all Israel with him took Achan the son of Zerah, and the silver and the cloak and the bar of gold, and his sons and daughters and his oxen and donkeys and sheep and his tent and all that he had. And they brought them up to the Valley of Achor. And Joshua said, "Why did you bring trouble on us? The LORD

brings trouble on you today." And all Israel stoned him with stones. They burned them with fire and stoned them with stones. And they raised over him a great heap of stones that remains to this day. Then the LORD turned from his burning anger. Therefore, to this day the name of that place is called the Valley of Achor. (Josh. 7:19–26)

It is a distressing scene. Achan and his family are lined up before the people of Israel—you can imagine the children looking at their father, asking, "Daddy, what are we doing here? Daddy, what have you done?"—and then they were stoned and their bodies burned.[1] It is a terrifying picture, and it is there to warn us that we cannot hide sin from the Lord. He sees our plans and intentions, He sees our evil deeds, and He knows.

There is judgment for those who will not repent and who imagine that sin will never catch up with them. There is a reckoning to come for every evil thought and every evil deed. Praise God that we have the opportunity to confess our sin to Him now, to turn from wrongdoing, and to find forgiveness through Jesus and His death in our place. But to imagine that we can hide our sin—to imagine that the Lord will not see—is pure folly.

I emphasize this because I know full well that some who are reading this book have hidden things in their life—things they hope are unknown to others and unnoticed by God. If that is the case for you, please do not be deceived. God knows and sees all things. You might think you have covered things well, you might think that the gold in your tent is well concealed, but the God of heaven sees all things and He knows all things. He cannot be fooled and He will not be mocked. If you have hidden sin in your life, deal with it honestly before the Lord. Confess it, turn from it, and find the forgiveness and grace that God extends in Jesus.

GOD HAS PERFECT KNOWLEDGE OF THE FUTURE

If, therefore, God has perfect knowledge of us, then the second point to make is that *He has perfect knowledge of the future*. In the world of business, plenty of analysts and economists are well versed in what is going on in the financial markets. They can analyze current events and explain them. But the people who gain acclaim and who gather vast fortunes are those who are able to predict where things will go in the future. That is the truly prized skill. But even the very best market forecasters are only right some of the time. No one actually knows what will happen tomorrow or next week, let alone next month or next year. Yet God is wonderfully distinct in this: He knows—He truly knows. It is one key characteristic that sets Him apart as the true and living God.

This distinctive of God is a major focus in the book of Isaiah. Just look at how the Lord speaks of Himself in Isaiah 44:

> "I am the first and I am the last;
>> besides me there is no god.
> Who is like me? Let him proclaim it.
>> Let him declare and set it before me,
> since I appointed an ancient people.
>> Let them declare what is to come, and what will happen.
> Fear not, nor be afraid;
>> have I not told you from of old and declared it?
>> And you are my witnesses!
> Is there a God besides me?
>> There is no Rock; I know not any." (Isa. 44:6–8)

And again:

> "Remember the former things of old;
>> for I am God, and there is no other;

I am God, and there is none like me,
declaring the end from the beginning
and from ancient times things not yet done,
saying, 'My counsel shall stand,
and I will accomplish all my purpose.'" (Isa. 46:9–10)

If any one fact about God compels me to believe that He is the true and living God, it is His proven ability to predict the future. If you are reading as a skeptic or an inquirer, I would love for you to engage with this key truth that sets Christianity apart from other religions. If you are reading as a believer wondering where to take a conversation with an unbelieving friend, let me commend this line of thought to you as centrally important. If you are reading as someone going through a time of doubt in your faith, let me invite you to be reassured as we think about this together.

Consider how it is that God has spoken to us and made Himself known. It is a very interesting thing that God chose to make Himself known to us through sixty-six different books, written by a large number of different authors, composed over a period of many centuries. In some ways, it might have seemed simpler just to give us one single download of divine revelation at one point in history, perhaps recorded by just one person in one neat document. God could have done that. But He chose instead to give us a diverse set of books, all inspired by Him as His Word, but penned by many authors in many locations over many hundreds of years.

That is a stark contrast to the models of revelation we see in other belief systems. I often think of the difference from Islam, where revelation is believed to have come to one particular person, through one particular event, when, alone in a cave, Muhammad is understood to have received foundational revelation. Now, as we consider that, it is very difficult to test or verify a claim to revelation received by one person in a cave on his own, or even by one person over the course of a single lifetime. But how different is the shape of Christian revelation. Woven into Christian revelation is the predictive prophecy given by God through a variety of people in different times and places. What we have in the Scriptures is a wonderful, repeated cycle of God making Himself known and saying what He will do and then, in time and space and human history, doing what He said He would do. Again and again He fulfilled His promises on the public and open pages of human history. This enables us to check His track record and to see if it all rings true. We get to analyze the data ourselves and, wonderfully, as we go through the Scriptures and travel through the centuries of God's many cycles of promise and fulfillment, we find that His Word is true and His promises are accurate.

ONE FULFILLED PROMISE OF GOD

If this book were a study of God's fulfilled promises, we could look in detail at the many different promises God made to His people and His enemies and see their accomplishment. As it is not, and in order to not distract from the main point of this chapter, I will pause to consider just one fulfilled promise, albeit the most wonderful one of all: the promise of a Savior who would come.

Right from the beginning of history the Lord promised that a deliverer would come to rescue His people from the problem of sin—their guilt before Him, and the judgment to come. As the Old Testament progressed, the promises grew in detail and particularity. Promise after promise was given. One of the most famous is found in Isaiah 53:

> He was despised and rejected by men,
>> a man of sorrows and acquainted with grief;

and as one from whom men hide their faces
  he was despised, and we esteemed him not.

Surely he has borne our griefs
  and carried our sorrows;
yet we esteemed him stricken,
  smitten by God, and afflicted.
But he was pierced for our transgressions;
  he was crushed for our iniquities;
upon him was the chastisement that brought us peace,
  and with his wounds we are healed. (Isa. 53:3–5)

The promise of a Savior who would come as a Servant and be pierced and crushed for our sin—a promise that speaks in such perfect detail of Jesus and His saving work—was written in the eighth century BC. Although it spoke of future events, our English translations render it in the past tense, signaling that because God had said it, it might as well already be history.

Volumes could be written examining how God made countless promises in His Word and fulfilled them on the very pages of human history—supremely, in the Son who came. His record in this demonstrates to us that His Word is true and entirely trustworthy. It shows us that He is the living God. "I am God, and there is none like me, declaring the end from the beginning and from ancient times things not yet done, saying, 'My counsel shall stand, and I will accomplish all my purpose'" (Isa. 46:9–10).

Each of us must eventually confront that basic question: Can I trust God's Word and rely on His promises? As we grapple with that—either in exploring the faith or in walking through a season of trial or doubt—hardly any more reassurance can be more powerful than to know that God has proved He knows and controls the future.

I tend to go through phases of trust and distrust when it comes to the weather forecast. I generally find the weather app on my phone to be pretty accurate, and so I am sometimes lulled into a sense of security and think that it can always be trusted. I remember looking at the app one day and seeing, with relief, that it was not predicting rain. Dark clouds were gathering outside the window, but I checked the app, and it still had no predication of rain. Then the heavens opened in a torrential downpour. The weather app did not even have the decency to admit that it was *now* raining. Scene outside: massive downpour. Picture on my phone: not a drop of rain.

It is a feature of our creatureliness that we do not know the future. But God knows all things and He knows what is to come. At the end of the day, that means that there is nothing more sensible or wise for me and you to do than simply to put our hand into the hand of Him who knows the future and entrust ourselves to Him. The way before us is dark to our eyes but the darkness is as light to Him. We can trust Him. He knows what lies ahead. He knows what the future holds. In fact, He controls the future, and has proved it time and time again. So, when He tells us in His Word that Jesus will return in glory; that He will save His people; that He will judge the wicked—when He makes promises like that—we can rely upon those promises and build our lives on them. We do well to listen to what He says.

Having considered God's perfect knowledge, I want to now turn to His perfect wisdom and consider, first, that *it is displayed supremely in Christ crucified*. It is one thing to know information; it is quite another to know how to use it well. To know how to make good decisions and good plans based on your knowledge— that is the heart of wisdom. The Scriptures tell us that God is not only supremely knowledgeable but also infinitely wise. Paul wrote that He is the "only wise God" (Rom. 16:27), while Job insisted, "With God are wisdom and might; he has counsel and understanding" (Job 12:13).

We could think pretty widely from Scripture about the wisdom of God, but I would like to focus on what is the central outworking of God's wisdom in the Bible, the pinnacle and the chief display of His wise planning and wise action, the greatest self-expression of His perfect wisdom, that is, Christ crucified.

To see this, I would like to consider Paul's first letter to the Corinthians. Paul was aware that many in his contemporary society were impressed by what sounded like wise speech and clever teaching, and he was aware that by comparison the gospel message he preached sounded simple, even absurd, to unbelievers. So he opened his letter by writing:

> For the word of the cross is folly to those who are perishing, but to us who are being saved it is the power of God. For it is written, "I will destroy the wisdom of the wise, and the discernment of the discerning I will thwart." Where is the one who is wise? Where is the scribe? Where is the debater of this age? Has not God made foolish the wisdom of the world? For since, in the wisdom of God, the world did not know God through wisdom, it pleased God through the folly of what we preach to save those who believe. For Jews demand signs and Greeks seek wisdom, but we preach Christ crucified, a stumbling block to Jews and folly to Gentiles, but to those who are called, both Jews and Greeks, Christ the power of God and the wisdom of God. For the foolishness of God is wiser than men, and the weakness of God is stronger than men. (1 Cor. 1:18–25)

The world has its own wisdom, but God's thoughts and God's ways are higher than ours. His wisdom is supreme, even if it looks like foolishness to the world. It is an extraordinary thing to consider. Knowing all things and having power over all things, the supreme wisdom of God was displayed in this: His incarnate Son hanging on a Roman cross to pay the penalty of my wrongdoing and yours. The wisdom of the all-knowing and all-powerful God was showcased as His sinless Son suffered the agony of death in the place of the guilty. That is the wisdom of our God.

The world, in all *its* wisdom, does not get it. It did not then, and it does not now. But it pleases God, wrote Paul, to save those who believe the preaching of the gospel. It is so very unexpected. So surprising. Jews demand signs and Greeks want the highest wisdom from the best philosophers, but we preach Christ crucified. The message is a stumbling block to Jews and it is sheer foolishness to Gentiles, but for those whom God has called, it is God's own power and God's own wisdom.

If you and I had even a fraction of the power and knowledge of God, in our natural state we would do everything we could to use it for our own satisfaction and pleasure. I have little doubt of that. But with all the knowledge and all the power in the universe within Himself, what does God do? How does He harness all that to carry out His supremely wise plan? In the person of His Son, He became human, humbled Himself, suffered agony, and died a shameful and excruciating death as a criminal.

The aim of this book is to help you to get to know God better; to see Him as He truly is. Here, as we look on His wisdom at the cross, perhaps we gain the deepest insight of all the insights we can gain: the all-wise God displays and expresses His wisdom supremely in the agony and shame of the cross. It seems like utter foolishness to the darkened mind. It looks like a disaster and seems like a gargantuan mistake. Why would God's Son die? Why would His Messiah suffer? But here is wisdom beyond all wisdom. Here is power beyond all strength. Here is a display of the glorious wisdom of God like no other. This display of God's wisdom tells us that the mind of God is profoundly unlike ours. We would never think of His plan. It is strange to our mind. But the cross of Christ is wisdom. Jesus is Himself the very embodiment of the wisdom of God. To see that moves us to humility as we recognize how darkened our own understanding is. To see that moves us to praise as we begin to understand that God is so much higher, so much more wonderful, than we can fully grasp.

.

seven

THE OMNIPRESENT GOD

One of our greatest limitations as human beings is our inability to be in two places at once. We cannot be at the business meeting and the school play at the same hour of the day; we cannot be at the supermarket and the doctor's office simultaneously; we cannot be lying in bed yet present at the gym first thing in the morning; and, save some very innovative telecommuting, we cannot be both at work and at the beach at once.

Essential to our humanity is our limitation—our finitude—when it comes to space. This, however, is not so with God. In fact, the reverse is true. Essential to His divinity is His ability to be in all places at once; to be fully present everywhere there is to be. And essential to our trust in Him is the confidence that He is always with us. Without that belief, our confidence will waver and fear will soon take hold. In times of lostness, loneliness, abandonment, and anxiety, sometimes the simple and great truth we need to remember is that God really is with us, really is at hand. The confidence of God's omnipresence is the foundation of the believer's comfort in both life and death. David articulated this so beautifully in the memorable words of Psalm 139:7–10:

> Where shall I go from your Spirit?
>> Or where shall I flee from your presence?
> If I ascend to heaven, you are there!
>> If I make my bed in Sheol, you are there!
> If I take the wings of the morning
>> and dwell in the uttermost parts of the sea,
> even there your hand shall lead me,
>> and your right hand shall hold me.

I want to begin this chapter by setting out the basic contours of the truth of God's omnipresence and, once I have laid down the foundations, I would like to think about the practical implications. First, though, the core reality that *God is fully present everywhere.* When Paul was in Athens he saw idol worship taking place and he used the opportunity to begin a conversation on the nature of the true and living God. Addressing the crowd around him, he said:

> "Men of Athens, I perceive that in every way you are very religious. For as I passed along and observed the objects of your worship, I found also an altar with this inscription: 'To the unknown god.' What therefore you worship as unknown, this I proclaim to you. The God who made the world and everything in it, being Lord of heaven and earth, does not live in temples made by man, nor is he served by human hands, as though he needed anything, since he himself gives to all mankind life and breath and everything. And he made from one man every nation of mankind to live on all the face of the earth, having determined allotted

periods and the boundaries of their dwelling place, that they should seek God, and perhaps feel their way toward him and find him. Yet he is actually not far from each one of us, for 'In him we live and move and have our being'; as even some of your own poets have said, 'For we are indeed his off-spring.'" (Acts 17:22–28)

The true and living God, who has no limits to His being, who is infinite and great, who is the Creator and sustainer of all things, cannot be contained by little temples like the idols of the world can. No, He is truly present in all parts of His creation.

It is wonderful having the blessing of cellphone technology. Your phone and, with it, your email, social media, and news feed, follow you wherever you go. You need never be cut off or un-plugged. Never, that is, until you hit a dead zone and, suddenly, you realize that the signal has its limits. If you look at a cell coverage map of Canada, for instance, you quickly see that vast portions of the country are totally unreached by cellular signal. Perhaps you have discovered that the hard way. You have had that uncomfort-able experience of needing to make contact with someone, maybe trying to call a tow truck because your car has broken down, or calling or texting a loved one in a time of emergency, and dis-covering that you have no signal. Very suddenly we can go from feeling infinitely connected to feeling terribly alone.

"Where shall I go from your Spirit? Or where shall I flee from your presence?" asked David in Psalm 139. There is nowhere in all creation where we can flee the Lord's own presence. His map has no dead zone. He is present, quite literally, *everywhere*. "Am I [only] a God at hand . . . and not a God far away?" the Lord asked in Jeremiah. "Can a man hide himself in secret places so that I can-not see him? . . . Do I not fill heaven and earth?" (Jer. 23:23–24).

GOD'S FULL PRESENCE

As human beings, you and I can struggle to be fully present intellectually and emotionally, even where we are physically present in a particular place. Think of the distracted parent on social media at home, oblivious to the chaos unfolding around; the student daydreaming about the upcoming vacation during science class; the inattentive churchgoer glancing at his phone during the sermon. We all know that we can be physically present but mentally absent. When God is present, however, He is fully present, not limited in any way by distraction or frailty of any kind.

When we imagine God being everywhere and filling the universe, we could imagine that He somehow stretches himself out or dilutes Himself to be in all places at once, but the infinite God is not limited in that kind of a way. In fact, if we find ourselves wondering how God can stretch Himself to fill all things, it may reveal that our view of God is too small. Solomon had it right when he prayed to dedicate the temple, saying, "But will God indeed dwell on the earth? Behold, heavens and the highest heaven cannot contain you; how much less this house that I have built!" (1 Kings 8:27). The infinite God cannot be contained. He is immense and unlimited. Where He is, He is fully.

I understand that, for certain medical specialties, a hospital in my home city of Ottawa will be the designated center to service some very far-flung communities in the extreme north of the country. If there is an urgent need for a particular type of surgery, a doctor in Ottawa will be the on-call doctor for those towns and villages. A patient in need might rightly ask: "Is there a doctor on call?" The answer would be: "Yes, the doctor is available and is willing to see you. She covers this area and you can consult her on the phone, but it will be a five-hour flight to actually get her there." The doctor is on call, but she is not exactly *there*.

When it comes to the God who governs and upholds the entire universe, He is fully present throughout His vast domain. All the time. In every place. That is the foundation of this truth we need to understand. At the same time, in order to rightly understand this truth in light of all the relevant biblical teaching, we need to also see that *God is present in different ways in different situations.* That is, the experience of God's presence is different for different people at different times.

We see parallels to this, of course. The presence of a police officer is experienced quite differently by a violent criminal being cuffed and put into the back of a patrol car than it is experienced by the officer's child when he gets home at night. It is the same police officer, the same presence in a way, but a very different experience of that presence. Or, think of a famous performer or politician. Among a great crowd of people, that person is encountered in one way, distantly, from afar, but then the person goes backstage and talks with her close coworkers or friends and the experience is different. It is the same person, but a very different kind of encounter. God is present everywhere. He is fully present in all places, but different people in different situations at different times experience His presence in different ways.

To help us understand this more deeply, we might need to consider the shape of the whole Bible narrative. When God created Adam and Eve, they were able to enjoy His presence in a very intimate way. They enjoyed fellowship with Him right from the start. They lived in a garden that was, in a very real sense, a sanctuary. God came down and walked with Adam in the cool of the day. They had openness, relationship, and access, and with all that came the fullness of the blessings of God. As we can all attest, that happy state of affairs did not last. After Adam and Eve rebelled, they were defiled by their sin and no longer fit for the presence of a holy God. As a result, they were thrown out of the Garden, and cherubim with a flaming sword were put in place to guard the way back. Outside the Garden, God was still present in the world and He still oversaw what His created people were doing, but it was not the same as the intimate experience of fellowship in the Garden.

Nevertheless, God was not done with the idea of enjoying friendship and closeness with His people. This purpose was really at the heart of His design for Israel, which was to be a nation and community with the presence of God at its heart. The tabernacle in the wilderness and the temple in Jerusalem were meant to be places where God's presence would dwell in a special way—a way that was reminiscent of the Garden. To be sure, access would be limited and would involve sacrifice and ritual, but the intention was there, and promises throughout the Old Testament pointed to a time in the future when God's presence would spill out beyond the temple building.

GOD'S PERSONAL PRESENCE

Move forward in time to the arrival of Jesus Christ. As He came to earth, significant statements in the New Testament tell us that His arrival was all about bringing the presence of God to His people. Matthew's gospel says that Jesus would be called "Immanuel," which means "God with us" (Matt. 1:23). John, speaking of Jesus, wrote that "the Word became flesh and dwelt among us." The phrase "dwelt among us" quite literally means that He "tabernacled"—"pitched His tent"—among us. John went on, "We have seen his glory, glory as of the only Son from the Father, full of grace and truth" (John 1:14). John was saying that Jesus is the full embodiment of the divine presence, now here among us. As He died on the cross to pay the price for our guilt and to deal with the problem of our separation from God, the gospel writers tell us that the curtain of the temple was torn in two, opening up the sanctuary and declaring that the building was no longer needed as a meeting place with God.

God had now come to us in this very personal way in Jesus, but as Jesus returned to heaven, He promised to send His Holy Spirit, so that all those who belong to Him would become His temple as His Spirit came to live within them. So, for God's people now, He is truly with us in an intimate and life-giving way. God's presence comes as a gift for the blessing of His saved people, first through the tabernacle and the temple, then through the person of His Son and the gift of His Spirit.

God's presence can, however, be experienced in a very different way as He comes near to do the work of judgment. Talking of the day of judgment to come, the Lord said through the prophet Malachi, "I will draw near to you for judgment. I will be a swift witness against the sorcerers, against the adulterers, against those who swear falsely, against those who oppress the hired worker in his wages, the widow and the fatherless, against those who thrust aside the sojourner, and do not fear me" (Mal. 3:5). Without probing the history and details too much, this text gives us insights that are both interesting and unsettling. First, it tells us that the work of judging sin is not something that God outsources, as we might outsource some of the less pleasant tasks we face. No, God actively deals with sin and sinners. Second, it indicates that God's omnipresence extends to the place of judgment itself:

> And another angel, a third, followed them, saying with a loud voice, "If anyone worships the beast and its image and receives a mark on his forehead or on his hand, he also will drink the wine of God's wrath, poured full strength into the cup of his anger, and he will be tormented with fire and sulfur in the presence of the holy angels and in the presence

of the Lamb. And the smoke of their torment goes up forever and ever." (Rev. 14:9–11)

The everlasting punishment spoken of here is the awful punishment of hell itself. Notice that all this happens in the presence of
the holy angels and of the Lamb Himself. Now, if the Lord is truly
present everywhere in the universe, then it should not surprise us
that the Lord is present in the work of judgment.

We often think of hell as an exclusion from the presence of the
Lord, and we have good reason for that. Paul wrote, for instance,
that those who do not respond to the gospel "will suffer the punishment of eternal destruction, away from the presence of the Lord
and from the glory of his might" (2 Thess. 1:9). Is it not a con-
tradiction if the omnipresent God is active in judgment, even in
hell, but at the same time the wicked are shut out of His presence?
Well, no, because Scripture takes it for granted that God is present
everywhere, but He is present to different people in different situations in different ways. God is present to judge the wicked, even
in the place of ultimate punishment, but His presence there does
not bring blessing and life. Those who are judged are entirely cut
off from His blessings and the life that He gives and, in that sense,
He is absent from them.

R. C. Sproul wrote this on the frightening doctrine of hell:

> A breath of relief is usually heard when someone declares,
> "Hell is a symbol for separation from God." To be separated
> from God for eternity is no great threat to the impenitent
> person. The ungodly want nothing more than to be sep-
> arated from God. Their problem in hell will not be sepa-
> ration from God, it will be the presence of God that will
> torment them.[1]

The Puritan Stephen Charnock—who wrote a great tome on the attributes of God—summarized the dynamics of the presence of God in different places in this way:

> God is in heaven, in regard of the manifestation of his glory; in hell, by the expression of his justice; in the earth, by the discoveries of his wisdom, power, patience, and compassion; in his people, by the monuments of his grace; and in all, in regard of his substance. He fills hell with his severity, heaven with his glory, his people with his grace.[2]

That is a lot to take in, but it is the great truth that we are considering. God is fully present everywhere—truly omnipresent—and yet present in different situations in different ways. Having seen the big picture, I want to now take it down to the practical level: How does this doctrine affect our thinking and living?

In the first place, *God's omnipresence comforts us in our trials.* There is hardly anything worse than feeling abandoned. We all value solitude sometimes, but to be really isolated, without friends, company, companions, or helpers, is a terrifying thing. We are social creatures created for relationship. That is why the punishment of solitary confinement is particularly agonizing. Those who spend months, and even years, in solitary confinement inevitably feel something of their humanity being sapped and even slipping away. Being truly alone is dreadful, but even without being locked in a cell, we can feel terribly isolated for one reason or another. Many know something of that experience. For those who know and love the Lord, however, we have the assurance that His presence is always with us—not in some general or vague sense, but in the specific sense that He is with us to minister His grace to us, to help us, to comfort us, and to uphold us.

A one-man play, *Solitary Refinement*, tells the story of Richard

Wurmbrand, a Romanian preacher who was imprisoned by the Communist regime in his country, tortured, and placed in solitary confinement for many years. One of the most moving aspects of his story is the account he gives of the Lord's presence with him and of the fellowship he enjoyed with the Lord Jesus, even from the depths of his underground cell. Despite his isolation and the agonies he endured, he could speak of how the presence of the Lord was very real and tangible to him.

One of my favorite verses in the Bible is found in 2 Chronicles and I think the King James Version captures it particularly well: "For the eyes of the LORD run to and fro throughout the whole earth, to shew himself strong in the behalf of them whose heart is perfect toward him" (2 Chron. 16:9 KJV). His eyes go to and fro throughout the earth, just looking for opportunities to show Himself strong on the behalf of His people—those who love Him and are devoted to Him. What an amazing thought. What an amazing comfort. As we feel weak and face trials, God is actively looking out for opportunities to show His strength. You can imagine the coast guard scouring the coastal waters after a storm, looking for those in distress and for opportunities to help and save. The Lord is scouring the face of the earth, as it were, just looking for opportunities to show Himself strong for His people.

GOD'S COMFORTING PRESENCE

You may feel alone, but if you belong to Jesus you are never alone. He is always there to minister His grace. "When the righteous cry for help, the LORD hears and delivers them out of all their troubles. The LORD is near to the brokenhearted and saves the crushed in spirit" (Ps. 34:17–18). Again, "God is our refuge and strength, a very present help in trouble" (Ps. 46:1). It may be that you are walking through some deep valleys and dark trials at the present time. You may feel very isolated. It may seem that others have abandoned you in your distress. It may be that those who seek to help just cannot comfort you because your distress is too deep. Perhaps someone you trust has failed you and it seems there is no one left to whom you can turn. In such a time, the believer's simple but profound comfort is this: God is with you and He hears your cries. He is close to the brokenhearted; He is their refuge and strength and ever-present help.

Reflecting on this wonderful truth, A. W. Tozer wrote:

> The certainty that God is always near us, present in all
> parts of His world, closer to us than our thoughts, should
> maintain us in a state of high moral happiness most of the
> time. But not all the time. It would be less than honest
> to promise every believer continual jubilee and less than
> realistic to expect it. As a child may cry out in pain even
> when sheltered in its mother's arms, so a Christian may
> sometimes know what it is to suffer even in the conscious
> presence of God. . . . But all will be well. In a world like
> this tears have their therapeutic effects. The healing balm
> distilled from the garments of the enfolding Presence cures
> our ills before they become fatal. The knowledge that we
> are never alone calms the troubled sea of our lives and
> speaks peace to our souls.[3]

The truth that God is omnipresent encourages us in our trials. It also serves to *chasten us in our sin*. Proverbs tells us that "the eyes of the LORD are in every place, keeping watch on the evil and the good" (Prov. 15:3). Not only does God see the good things that happen in this world, He sees what the wicked do too. He sees the thoughts and intentions of our heart, so that everything is laid bare before Him as we saw earlier in Hebrews 4. When we are walking in rebellion and doing things that we would prefer no one saw, the sobering truth is that God is there, He sees, and He is watching.

For a long time a legend circulated that the writer Arthur Conan Doyle—best known, of course, for creating the character Sherlock Holmes—once sent a prank telegram to twelve leading figures in British society. The telegram was unsigned and simply read: "Flee! All is revealed." As the legend goes, within twenty-four hours, all twelve had left the country. Of course, none of us would want all our sin put on display. Sin flourishes in the darkness and we would be rightly ashamed to have every thought and deed seen and known by others. Yet the simple fact of the matter is that God always sees.

Many of us quickly acknowledge the truth of this. If God is God, He must see. But do we take that reality seriously enough? I think that if we really believed it, this truth would be a tremendous motivation for us to flee sin. Maybe you are engaged in patterns of behavior that you would be terribly ashamed for friends and family or Christian brothers and sisters to witness, but the omnipresent God is always there.

Sometimes even believers think they can keep God at a distance or can somehow outrun Him. Perhaps you are actively fleeing the Lord today. You believe He exists, you know that He has a call on your life, you may sense He is not pleased with the way in which you are living, but you are simply hoping you can keep Him at arm's length.

It has now been a quarter of a century since the famous white Bronco chase when American football star O. J. Simpson tried in vain to outrun the police who were pursuing him to arrest him for murder. The footage was broadcast all over the world. It was a totally hopeless exercise. Helicopters were watching from above, police were pursuing behind, and, no doubt, troopers were gathering farther ahead. But he tried to run. It was ridiculous, even absurd.

Do not fool yourself by thinking that you can outrun God or escape His claim on your life. Do not fool yourself by thinking that you can ultimately escape the demands of His justice. The very idea is absurd. If you are running away from the all-present God, why not run to Him instead?[4] Why not find the gracious welcome that He will give you through the Lord Jesus? He opens His arms to those who turn from rebellion and who come to Him in faith.

GOD'S ENABLING PRESENCE

The omnipresence of God comforts us in trials, chastises us in sin, and *enables us for our mission.* It is an awful thing to be sent to do a job without the proper support and help that you need. I have heard that a new radio system our local police force has just begun using is proving a little troublesome. Reception can be bad and officers report not being able to make contact with base in potentially dangerous situations. It could, of course, be disastrous to get into a tense situation and be unable to call for backup—to suddenly be isolated when you most need support.

Only a handful of citizens will be sent into the community in the name of law and order, but all of us who follow Jesus are sent into the world in His name. It can be very daunting. We can find ourselves in immensely challenging situations as we serve, but the Bible tells us that when the Lord calls us to go and do His work and proclaim His Word, He will never send us out alone. Moses discovered that truth in his day when the Lord sent him to bring about the release of His people from slavery in Egypt. In Exodus 3, the Lord appeared to Moses in the burning bush—a great manifestation of the presence of God—and told him that He would send him to Pharaoh to bring the Israelites out of Egypt. Moses asked the reasonable question, "Who am I that I should go to Pharaoh and bring the children of Israel out of Egypt?" (v. 11).Who am I to do this? I do not have the capacity, the gifts, the resources, or the courage. Who am I to go out and understand this great work? God's response is as simple as it is sufficient, "I will be with you" (v. 12).

That is it. That is enough. You, an unknown farmer's helper from Midian, are going to walk into the throne room of the most powerful man in the world and demand that he set free hundreds of thousands of valuable slaves. How will you do it? How is this going to work? How can this make any sense? "I will be with you."

Many centuries later Jesus gave His disciples—and the church—marching orders for a very great mission, "All authority in heaven and on earth has been given to me. Go therefore and make disciples of all nations, baptizing them in the name of the Father and of the Son and of the Holy Spirit, teaching them to observe all that I have commanded you" (Matt. 28:18–20). It is a tall order. The world very often does not want to hear the word of Jesus. It does not appreciate being called to obey. In our contemporary culture, living out this commission can bring social embarrassment and charges of narrow-mindedness. In other parts of the world, proclaiming the word of Jesus can lead to imprisonment or death. We are not even naturally good at it. We so often do not know what to say. We do not have the courage we need, and our own personal witness is very often unimpressive. *Who are we to go? Who are we to speak?*

The Great Commission encompasses our home, teaching our children the truth; our community, sharing the gospel with peers, colleagues, and friends; and our church, serving in the various roles God gives us. As the Lord sends us out into the world to do His Great Commission work—to make disciples of all nations—we can feel entirely overwhelmed by the magnitude of the task, heavily burdened by a sense of our own insufficiency. If we take the task seriously, we must feel something of that. But notice how Jesus finishes His commission: "I am with you always, to the end of the age" (Matt. 28:20). Here is the strengthening truth: the

Lord Jesus is with us by His Spirit and He is helping us. His presence is what makes it possible for each of us to play our part in our own context. It is what will make it possible for you to summon the energy to read the Scriptures with your kids tonight, as you go once again into the hostile workplace or classroom tomorrow, and as you gear up for another evening of small group ministry. The omnipresent Lord is with us—truly with us—to help and strengthen and direct us.

Finally, and more briefly, I want to close this chapter by considering that the promise of the presence of God *fills us with hope for the future*. For the Christian believer, our central hope is that we will be with the Lord in the life to come. Our experience of His presence will be richer and deeper than our experience thus far, and being with Him will bring us fullness of joy. The psalmist expresses this longing. "One thing have I asked of the LORD, that will I seek after: that I may dwell in the house of the LORD all the days of my life, to gaze upon the beauty of the LORD and to inquire in his temple" (Ps. 27:4). If we know and love the Lord, we want to be with Him. The great hope of the gospel and the great promise of the Scriptures is that we will indeed be with Him one day. We will dwell in His house and gaze upon the beauty of His holiness. Wonderfully, we have the Spirit living within us even now and have access to the Father through the Son. But there is a greater reality to come and a fuller experience of the presence of God.

And I heard a loud voice from the throne saying, "Behold, the dwelling place of God is with man. He will dwell with them, and they will be his people, and God himself will be with them as their God. He will wipe away every tear from their eyes, and death shall be no more, neither shall there be mourning, nor crying, nor pain anymore, for the former things have passed away." (Rev. 21:3–4)

That is the very heart of the Christian hope. We will experience the presence of this omnipresent God in a richer and fuller way in a day to come. We will experience the blessing and joy of His presence in a way we have not yet known. This is why, of course, the final prayer of the Bible is simply this, "Come, Lord Jesus!" (Rev. 22:20).

A very dear friend wrote to me recently. He has been going through a terrible time of trial and disappointment and sadness. It is a dark valley. He gave me an update on his situation and finished his message simply by repeating that verse, "Come, Lord Jesus." We want Him to come so that we can be with Him. In the midst of the sadness and grief that we experience in this life, this is the ultimate hope that sustains us. One day we will see our Savior face to face, and in that day all will truly be well.

eight

THE GLORIOUS GOD

Thousands gather across cities in Canada every July to watch spectacular fireworks light up the night sky to mark Canada Day—just as thousands gather in Washington to see the nation's military power on display in honor of Independence Day. When we lived in the UK, we would watch crowds gather and jostle to catch a glimpse of a royal wedding or jubilee celebration in all its pomp and grandeur.

We long to see and experience something great and majestic, something beyond the ordinary, something of significance and worth. We are naturally hungry for glory. We are attracted to glory; we seek it. The theme of this final chapter is glory—not the fading glory of this world, but the true glory belonging only to God Himself.

With each attribute of God that we consider and explore, it is good for us to pause and ask the question: What will I lack in my Christian life if I fail to grasp this truth about God? In what way will I be diminished in my discipleship, hampered in my godliness, held back in my devotion? We have attempted, in different ways, to answer that question in each chapter. We will give consideration to it in this chapter in more detail below. But because the point is so pressing and so significant, I would like to suggest an interim answer to the question, even before we really begin. I want to suggest that if we do not understand and grasp the truth that God is truly glorious, we are in grave danger of misdirecting the affection of our hearts, the ambition of our dreams, and the energy of our lives. The Christian life is driven and inspired in a very real sense by a God-given vision of His great glory.

This was the experience of the prophet Isaiah in his call to ministry. God gave him a vision of His own glory—and that vision shaped all that Isaiah did for the rest of his life. That vision set Isaiah on the path to being the great servant and prophet of God that he proved to be. Just picture the scene that Isaiah was privileged to behold:

> In the year that King Uzziah died I saw the Lord sitting upon a throne, high and lifted up; and the train of his robe filled the temple. Above him stood the seraphim. Each had six wings: with two he covered his face, and with two he covered his feet, and with two he flew. And one called to another and said:
>
> "Holy, holy, holy is the LORD of hosts;
> the whole earth is full of his glory!"
>
> And the foundations of the thresholds shook at the voice of him who called, and the house was filled with smoke. (Isa. 6:1–4)

Having given Isaiah that vision, the Lord then asked who would go out for Him and serve Him. "Whom shall I send, and who will go for us?" (v. 8). Having seen this vision of the Lord in His glory, Isaiah was ready to respond and to go, "Here I am! Send me" (v. 8).

The vision of the Lord in His glory reshaped and redirected Isaiah's life. It set him on the path to a life of extraordinary service, devotion, and fruitfulness. It is no exaggeration to say that we need a biblical vision of God's glory to be stamped upon our hearts and minds if we are to enjoy and experience anything of the like in our lives.

GOD IS ENTIRELY GLORIOUS

Although we could take a varied approach to this wonderful attribute, for clarity and concision I will focus on two points, and the first is that *God is entirely glorious.* This is a truth that is proclaimed, celebrated, and wondered at throughout the Scriptures. Imagining God in His glory entering Jerusalem, David cried out in Psalm 24:

> Lift up your heads, O gates!
>   And be lifted up, O ancient doors,
>   That the King of glory may come in.
> Who is this King of glory?
>   The LORD, strong and mighty,
>   the LORD, mighty in battle!
> Lift up your heads, O gates!
>   And lift them up, O ancient doors,
>   that the King of glory may come in.
> Who is this King of glory?
>   The LORD of hosts,
>   he is the King of glory! (vv. 7–10)

The language of "glory" is used a lot in the Bible and it is used in a variety of ways. But at the most fundamental level, it speaks of the excellence of God Himself: His worth and His beauty, the perfection of His character, His holiness, and power. "Glory" refers in a basic way to the excellence of God, but this language is also used to speak of the visible display of God's worth and majesty. It indicates the fact that this majestic and holy God is manifestly present.

When the people of Israel traveled away from slavery in Egypt toward the promised land, God's glory was present and visible to them in the cloud that led them by day and the pillar of fire that led them by night. When Moses met with God at Mount Sinai, God was present there in His glory, and the cloud and the fire were the physical manifestations of His presence:

> Then Moses went up on the mountain, and the cloud covered the mountain. The glory of the LORD dwelt on Mount Sinai, and the cloud covered it six days. And on the seventh day he called to Moses out of the midst of the cloud. Now the appearance of the glory of the LORD was like a devouring fire on the top of the mountain in the sight of the people of Israel. Moses entered the cloud and went up on the mountain. And Moses was on the mountain forty days and forty nights. (Ex. 24:15–18)

Later in the book of Exodus, the Israelites sinned greatly by making and worshiping the golden calf while Moses was on the mountain meeting with the Lord. The Lord had been gracious in not casting off His people nor revoking His promise to continue to go with them. Moses then made a great request, asking, "Please show me your glory" (Ex. 33:18). The Lord put Moses in a cleft in the rock and covered him while He passed by, stipulating, "Then I will take away my hand, and you shall see my back, but my face shall not be seen" (Ex. 33:23).

Moses knew that seeing and experiencing the glory of God would be a majestic, awe-inspiring thing. That is what he longed for; that is what he asked for. And, quite incredibly, the Lord said that He would make His character and identity known to Moses

and the people in a special way. He would show them His goodness, proclaim His name, have mercy on sinners, and show compassion on the needy. Those are all aspects of His glory and they reveal
the beauty and wonder of who He is. But a full, unfiltered display
of that glory would be too much for Moses. In fact, it would be
too much for anyone. Nonetheless, Moses was given a partial and
limited display, shielded from a distance. In Moses's desire to see
God's glory there is a wholesome and appropriate longing. God's
glory is wonderful, and seeing Him as He is would be magnificent.
But God's reaction teaches us that it is not quite that easy for sinful
people to see His unfiltered glory.

Another figure from the Old Testament who learned something
of this lesson, and who saw something of the Lord's glory, was the
prophet Isaiah. We considered already the great vision he received
at his commissioning (Isa. 6:1–4). When he saw the powerful manifestation of the Lord's presence he immediately cried, "Woe to me!
For I am lost; for I am a man of unclean lips, and I dwell in the
midst of a people of unclean lips; for my eyes have seen the King,
the LORD of hosts" (v. 5). In that moment, it seems, Isaiah realized
that the Lord is so great, so holy, and so majestic that compared to
Him, he himself was grossly tainted and defiled by sin. The only
result of such exposure, he reasoned, would be his ruin and destruction. It is akin to approaching the inner chamber of a nuclear
reactor, in that the sheer radiance of energy is more than any one of
us could safely absorb in our natural state.

JESUS REVEALS THE GLORY OF GOD

The Old Testament, then, reveals God as entirely glorious, but
also as unapproachable in His glory. It shows that His glory is too
bright, too radiant, too pure for sinners like us to approach. Of
course, the New Testament picks up on this theme, but it shows

us that, in the coming of Jesus, something radical and wonderful has taken place.

A verse that I continue to return to when I think about the attributes of God is found at the start of John's gospel. It is one of the most important verses bridging the Old Testament and the New. Referring tò Jesus, John wrote, "And the Word became flesh and dwelt among us, and we have seen his glory, glory as of the only Son from the Father, full of grace and truth" (John 1:14). Moses longed to see the glory of God, but God told him he could not do so and live. Isaiah saw something of the Lord in His glory in a vision, but he feared he would be consumed by the display. But now, in Jesus we have seen the glory of God. As the Son became flesh in the incarnation, the glorious God came to us in a way that we could see and know Him, without us being consumed by the sheer radiance of His holiness.

The revelation of the glory of God in the person and work of Jesus is a theme that John in particular explored and developed in his gospel. John wanted us to see that as we watch and listen to Jesus, there is a revealing of the very glory of God. When Jesus performed His first miracle in chapter 2, turning water into wine at the wedding at Cana, John wrote, "This, the first of his signs, Jesus did at Cana in Galilee, and manifested his glory. And his disciples believed in him" (John 2:11). The miracles of Jesus reveal His glory and give us a window into His majesty, power, and beauty. Yet as the gospel account progressed, Jesus made it clear that the true moment of glory—the moment when His glory would be revealed most profoundly and radiantly—would be as He died on the cross.

In chapter 12, Jesus gave one of the most significant predictions of His death:

"The hour has come for the Son of Man to be glorified. Truly, truly, I say to you, unless a grain of wheat falls into the earth and dies, it remains alone; but if it dies, it bears much fruit. Whoever loves his life loses it, and whoever hates his life in this world will keep it for eternal life. If anyone serves me, he must follow me; and where I am, there will my servant be also. If anyone serves me, the Father will honor him.

"Now is my soul troubled. And what shall I say? 'Father, save me from this hour'? But for this purpose I have come to this hour. Father, glorify your name." Then a voice came from heaven: "I have glorified it, and I will glorify it again." (John 12:23–28)

What is the moment of "glorification" according to John? When would the glory of God shine most clearly through the person and work of Jesus? It is at the cross, where the kernel of wheat fell to the ground and died to give life to many. It is at the cross, the place of torment from which Jesus might have asked to be saved. He came for that hour because the Father's name would be revealed as glorious, lifted up and exalted, as the Son died for sinners like us.

It is worth pausing for a moment to take this in. God is glorious—radiant in power and majesty and holiness and goodness. He is so glorious that Moses could not look on His glory without being destroyed. But in Jesus, through the miracle of the incarnation, we have now seen the glory of God. We have seen His glory in the miracles He performed and the words He spoke, but this revelation of glory reached its pinnacle at the very moment when God the Son died in agony and humility for the sin of His people.

What does this say about our glorious God and His character and nature? If that is the moment of the revelation of the glory of God, what kind of God is this? If the ugliness and agony and shame of the cross is the glory of the all-glorious God, then who is this God we worship and this Lord we adore? He is the God of mercy and compassion, of grace and justice. He is the God of love untold, of grace unfathomable. He is the God whose glory it is to die for His rebellious, lost, and hopeless creatures. He is the God whose radiant glory is revealed as He gives His one and only Son for you and for me.

Our God is the God of glory. I wonder if you know Him? I wonder if, with the eyes of faith, you have seen Him in His glory in the person of His Son? I wonder if the sheer radiance of His glory has transformed your life and shone into your heart? If you do not know Him, you can know Him. If you have not come to Him, you can come to Him. You do it by trusting in His Son and receiving the love and grace and mercy He poured out at the cross. That is, quite simply, the offer of the gospel and it is for you and for me. It is for all who will believe.

Beautiful things can be found in this world, things that have a certain glory about them. Not long ago, my wife and I were doing a little window shopping downtown, and we wandered into Tiffany's and saw all the beautiful things sparkling in the display cases. A beautiful jewel that has been well cut and shown in the right light can be a breathtaking thing. But there is no such thing as a truly flawless jewel. Not even the finest diamond in the display cases at Tiffany's can be said to be without flaw or fault. Diamonds are graded, in part, on their clarity and their lack of imperfection, and you can find some that are very close to perfect. But the totally flawless diamond, totally clear, totally brilliant, completely unmarred—does not exist.

WE EXIST TO BRING GOD GLORY

In contrast, God is flawless in His perfections, His beauty, His holiness, His goodness, power, wisdom, and knowledge. He is truly glorious in every way. That is the core idea of this chapter, and I do not think it is too hard to take on board. If we believe in God—if we trust in Him—we understand and accept that He is truly the God of glory. What, then, do we do with this truth? Well, if God is all-glorious, then *our purpose is to bring Him glory.* That is where this truth leads us.

What is the purpose of my life? It is an agonizing question that we all must ask from time to time. The Centers for Disease Control and Prevention recently issued a startling report showing that suicide rates over the last decade or so have been rising in almost every American state.[1] It raises the question of causation—of why it has been happening—and, of course, numerous factors feed into this troubling trend. But I was interested to read an opinion piece in the *New York Times* by a behavioral scientist that seemed to offer substantial insight:

> Many argue that this is a crisis of mental health care, that people are not getting the services they need. The proposed solution is better therapies, more effective antidepressants and greater access to treatment.
>
> This assessment may be correct. However, the suicide rate has increased even as more people are seeking treatment for depression and anxiety, and even as treatment for those conditions has become more widely available. An additional explanation seems to be needed.
>
> As a behavioral scientist who studies basic psychological needs, including the need for meaning, I am convinced that our nation's suicide crisis is in part a crisis of meaninglessness. . . .
>
> We are a species that strives not just for survival, but also for significance. We want lives that matter. . . .
>
> A felt lack of meaning in one's life has been linked to alcohol and drug abuse, depression, anxiety and—yes—

suicide. And when people experience loss, stress or trauma, it is those who believe that their lives have a purpose who are best able to cope with and recover from distress.[2]

What is the purpose of my life; where is meaning to be found? These are vitally important questions. In fact, you may be reading this today because you are exploring precisely these questions. Well, the Bible does not have a one-line answer. There is not a single verse we can point to that sums it all up. But if we look at the whole teaching of Scripture—at the whole shape of what God has made known to us—then the answer emerges pretty quickly: the Lord makes it clear throughout His Word that the heart of His purpose in all things is for His glory to be seen and acknowledged and reflected by the people He has made.

In a very interesting passage in Isaiah, the Lord spoke of how He was refraining from bringing upon Israel a judgment the nation deserved because of its sin, and He explained why He was doing this. We might imagine that He would say that He was acting in this way for the sake of the people, out of love and compassion for them. That would make good sense to us. Instead, He said He was actually doing it for His own sake and for the sake of His glory:

> For my name's sake I defer my anger;
>> for the sake of my praise I restrain it for you,
>> that I may not cut you off.
> Behold, I have refined you, but not as silver;
>> I have tried you in the furnace of affliction.
> For my own sake, for my own sake, I do it,
>> for how should my name be profaned?
>> My glory I will not give to another. (Isa. 48:9–11)

God will not have His glory diminished and His reputation defamed through the shame and destruction of His own covenant people, Israel. And so, for the sake of His reputation and His glory among the nations of the earth, He held back His judgment upon His people.

God is rightly concerned for His glory. He is truly glorious, and it is fitting that His glory should be seen. Throughout the Scriptures, His true people recognize that He is worthy of all glory. Look at the way in which the Psalms express this desire and concern:

> Ascribe to the LORD, O families of the peoples,
>> ascribe to the LORD glory and strength!
> Ascribe to the LORD the glory due his name;
>> bring an offering, and come into his courts!
> Worship the LORD in the splendor of holiness;
>> tremble before him, all the earth! (Ps. 96:7–9)

And again,

> I will give thanks to you, O LORD, among the peoples;
>> I will sing praises to you among the nations.
> For your steadfast love is great above the heavens;
>> your faithfulness reaches to the clouds.
> Be exalted, O God, above the heavens!
>> Let your glory be over all the earth! (Ps. 108:3–5)

And yet again,

> Not to us, O LORD, not to us, but to your name give glory,
>> for the sake of your steadfast love and your faithfulness!
> (Ps. 115:1)

The Westminster Shorter Catechism, a famous summary of the faith, expresses this particularly well. The catechism asks: "What is the chief end of man?" (Or, to put it in today's language: "What is the main purpose of humanity?") The chief end of man, the catechism says, is "To glorify God, and to enjoy him forever." In other words, our chief purpose is to return glory to the glorious God and to enjoy the God who is thoroughly glorious.[3]

Overall, I think that is a good summary of the Bible's teaching, and, from what we have already seen in this chapter, it makes sense. God is supremely wonderful and truly glorious. He is the great jewel, the Being of supreme worth at the heart of the universe. It makes sense that everything should revolve around Him and His glory.

THE WORLD EXISTS TO BRING GOD GLORY

The Centre Block of Canada's Parliament building is an altogether attractive and imposing edifice, but I think the most beautiful part of it is the parliamentary library. The library is the only part of the building that survived the great fire of 1916, and dates back to the nineteenth century. If you have had the opportunity to visit the library, you will know what a striking room it is—a great open rotunda with galleries spanning the circumference and a towering statue of Queen Victoria in the center, in the place of absolute preeminence. It is my understanding that the base of Queen Victoria's statue goes right down to the foundation of the building, even as she rises to height within the room. The point is that the Queen is at the center of everything in Victorian Canada. The institution of government and the Dominion itself are grounded in her rule and exist for her good pleasure. The symbolism is both powerful and inescapable.

There is a sense in which the world, and indeed the universe, is a great gallery built around the King of glory Himself. The great jewel of the glory of God shines at the center and everything is about Him, calculated to reflect His majesty and splendor. You may remember how Psalm 19 begins, "The heavens declare the glory of God, and the sky above proclaims his handiwork" (Ps. 19:1). It is all for Him. All for His glory.

Despite what we may think, the universe is not all about us. To recognize this is humbling, but it is also wholesome and good because once we grasp it, it leads to true joy. Remember again what the catechism says, "The chief end of man is to glorify God and enjoy him forever." Glorifying God and finding joy in God go hand in hand. Ultimately it is only as we find purpose and meaning in glorifying the One who is truly glorious that we find lasting joy. Augustine said, "You have made us for yourself, and our heart is restless until it rests in you."[4] We were made for God, and nothing other than Him will satisfy us. Some might charge that God is somehow egotistical or unduly selfish to make a universe centered on His glory, but we only think that way when we fail to recognize that God Himself is the only One who is truly glorious, the only One who can ever satisfy the longings of our soul, and the only One who can bring true and lasting joy.

When I was younger, I used to sing a chorus at a Christian camp—"All that I need is in Jesus; he satisfies; joy he supplies; life would be worthless without him; all things in Jesus I find."[5] It is a simple song, but it holds such good truth to sing and to remember. If you and I do not see and recognize that the universe is built around God and is for His glory, the alternative is that we will seek to find meaning elsewhere, and, if we do that, we will find ourselves at the heart of what the Bible calls idolatry. We replace worship of the true and living God with the worship of an alternative god of our own choosing. The results are always disastrous.

Timothy Keller, in considering the theme of idolatry, memorably cites a college commencement speech given by David Foster Wallace, an American writer and intellectual who later took his own life.[6] I think Foster Wallace's remarks in that address are poignant, not least because he was evidently grappling deeply with these things himself as an unbeliever.

> Everybody worships. The only choice we get is what to worship. And the compelling reason for maybe choosing some sort of god . . . to worship . . . is that pretty much anything else you worship will eat you alive. If you worship money and things, if they are where you tap real meaning in life, then you will never have enough, never feel you have enough. It's the truth. Worship your own body and beauty and sexual allure and you will always feel ugly. And when time and age start showing, you will die a million deaths before [your loved ones] finally grieve you. . . . Worship power, and you will end up feeling weak and afraid, and you will need ever more power over others to numb you to your own fear. Worship your intellect, being seen as smart, you will end up feeling stupid, a fraud, always on the verge of being found out. But the insidious thing about these forms of worship is not that they are evil or sinful; it is that they're unconscious. They are default settings.[7]

There is a man who did not have a Christian faith but who saw the issue so clearly. The worship of anything other than the true and living God is not only unsatisfying but it is also destructive.

Foster Wallace was hardly the only person to recognize the futility of these pursuits. Henry Patterson, who wrote under the pen name Jack Higgins, was one of the world's bestselling authors. He wrote more than eighty books that have sold a combined total of 150 million copies. He reached the top of his field. Patterson was once asked if there was anything he wished someone had told his younger self. His answer was simply this: he wished someone had told him that when you get to the top, there is nothing there.

Alexander the Great was made king at twenty. He sought to increase his empire through war and was undefeated in battle. By thirty, he had created one of the greatest empires the world has ever seen. Legend has it that when he conquered so much of the known world, he looked out at his realm and wept because there was not another world for him to conquer. I do not know if the legend is true, but it is entirely believable. Nothing in this world can satisfy, not even the world itself.

"You have made us for yourself, O Lord, and our hearts are restless until they find their rest in you."

We are restless, empty, and misdirected until our hearts find their rest in God—the One whose glory is limitless and entirely satisfying. Do you know that meaning in your life today? Have you been out hunting glory anywhere and everywhere, seeking satisfaction and fullness in the things of this world? Perhaps you have enjoyed a measure of success, but ultimately you found those things empty and lacking. If you have, the invitation of the gospel and the call of Jesus Christ is to come to Him to find true meaning and purpose and, with those things, wholeness and joy. Our worship of idols is a culpable thing before God, making us guilty in His sight. But Jesus died to pay the penalty of our idolatry and all our wrongdoing. He shows us the glory of the true and living God and calls us to reorient our lives around His glory, away from the glory of our little idols, which can never satisfy nor bear the weight of our worship.

Perhaps you know and trust the Lord Jesus, but as you consider God's glory, you realize that you have been living again for petty little idols. You have been wandering in your worship and glory-hunting elsewhere, even though you know better. Perhaps as you reflect on this attribute of God you realize that there are some things you need to make right, some idolatry of which you need to repent. You need to be consumed once again with zeal for the glory of God and with delight in who He is.

For those who know the Lord, He holds in store a glorious future. He is glorious and He has made us to reflect and enjoy His glory. That is what awaits us if we belong to Jesus. Describing the New Jerusalem to come, John wrote:

> I saw no temple in the city, for its temple is the Lord God the Almighty and the Lamb. And the city has no need of sun or moon to shine on it, for the glory of God gives it light, and its lamp is the Lamb. By its light will the nations walk, and the kings of the earth will bring their glory into it. (Rev. 21:22–24)

If we recognize how radiantly beautiful the Lord is in His power, majesty, holiness, and splendor, then the picture John gave us should fill our hearts with wonder and delight. We will live forever basking in the radiance of the glory of God. What a prospect. What a future. What a God.

KNOWING GOD THROUGH HIS ATTRIBUTES

A t different times in our lives, we might express our spiritual and intellectual need in different ways. We might sense a need to understand better the problem of suffering, the dynamics of Christian ethics in a complex world, the hope of heaven, the interpretation of biblical prophecy, or a whole host of other theological topics. All these are worthy of our consideration, study, and reflection. Undoubtedly there are plenty of books on the marketplace to help us explore each of those topics. But the truth is that our deepest and most fundamental need is simply and profoundly this: to know God better. Over the years I have observed that many churches have taken as their mission statement the simple aim, "To know God and make Him known." It is indeed simple, but there is something wonderfully right about it.

God has been gracious enough to make Himself known to us in the Scriptures and in the person of Jesus Christ. He has spoken to us; He has revealed Himself to us. And Jesus teaches us that the essence of true life is to know Him (John 17:3). When we struggle in our understanding of truth and in our personal discipleship, our deepest need is always that we would know God better. The connection between personal knowledge of God and godly living is more vital and essential than we might realize. Consider, for example, John's insistence that love must characterize the person who has come to know the God who is love. The connection is unbreakable as he expresses it: "Beloved, let us love one another, for love is from God, and whoever loves has been born of God and knows God. Anyone who does not love does not know God, because God is love" (1 John 4:7–8). If we know God, our lives will be shaped by who He is.

Ultimately, this is the goal and the outcome of our study of the Scriptures; it is the goal when we hear the Word of God taught and proclaimed. In a very moving passage in 2 Corinthians 3, Paul wrote of the privilege that was his to proclaim Christ as a minister of the new covenant. He contrasted his privilege with that of Moses under the old covenant, and delighted in the wonder of what takes place as Christ is proclaimed now—"And we all, with unveiled face, beholding the glory of the Lord, are being transformed into the same image from one degree of glory to another. For this comes from the Lord who is the Spirit" (v. 18).

When Christ is proclaimed from His Word, we see something of the glory of the Lord; and when we behold the Lord's glory, the Spirit transforms His people into the likeness of Christ, that we might reflect something of His unique glory. If we would trust the Lord, delight in the Lord, and grow to be like the Lord, then this much is essential: we must know the Lord. The centrality of this—the worth of this—was something that the apostle Paul grasped in a profound way, so much so that he was able to attest from his heart, "Indeed, I count everything as loss because of the surpassing worth of knowing Christ Jesus my Lord" (Phil. 3:8).

It is my prayer that this study has helped you to know the Lord better—even to *see* something of His glorious character through His Word—and that this deepening knowledge of Him will be of surpassing worth to you and will lead to life transformation in the power of His Spirit.

NOTES

CHAPTER 1: THE ETERNAL GOD

1. In the outline of the essentials of this truth in this section, I am indebted particularly to Wayne Grudem's treatment of it in his *Systematic Theology* (Grand Rapids: Zondervan, 1994), 168–73.

2. Matthew Barrett draws upon Stephen Charnock for this image. See Barrett, *None Greater: The Undomesticated Attributes of God* (Grand Rapids: Baker Books, 2019), 147.

3. Isaac Watts, "O God, Our Help in Ages Past," Hymnary.org, 1719, https://hymnary.org/text/our_god_our_help_in_ages_past_watts.

4. Beeke and Smalley's suggestions of key applications of this doctrine are immensely helpful and have been instructive in shaping the lines of application I develop here. Joel R. Beeke and Paul M. Smalley, *Reformed Systematic Theology: Revelation and God*, vol. 1 (Wheaton, IL: Crossway, 2019), 666–70.

5. Thomas Watson, *A Body of Divinity* (Edinburgh: The Banner of Truth Trust, 1983), 61.

6. Watson, *Body of Divinity*, 65.

7. C. S. Lewis, *Collected Letters*, ed. Walter Hooper, vol. 3, *Narnia, Cambridge, and Joy 1950–1963* (New York: HarperCollins, 2007), 76.

CHAPTER 3: THE UNCHANGING GOD

1. Walter Chalmers Smith, "Immortal, Invisible, God Only Wise," Hymnary.org, 1867, https://hymnary.org/text/immortal_invisible_god_only_wise.
2. Lynn Taylor, cited in Jacquelyn Smith, "How to Manage a Moody Boss," *Forbes*, June 25, 2013, https://www.forbes.com/sites/jacquelyn smith/2013/06/25/how-to-manage-a-moody-boss/?sh=e6217cd330a3.
3. J. C. Ryle, *Holiness* (Darlington, England: Evangelical Press, 1979), xvii.
4. "Support for Same-Sex Marriage Grows, Even Among Groups That Had Been Skeptical," Pew Research Center, June 26, 2017, https://www.pewresearch.org/politics/2017/06/26/support-for-same-sex-marriage-grows-even-among-groups-that-had-been-skeptical.
5. John Dick, cited in A. W. Pink, *The Attributes of God* (Grand Rapids: Baker Books, 1975), 50.

CHAPTER 4: THE INDEPENDENT GOD

1. Jonathan Edwards, "Discourse on the Trinity," *The Works of Jonathan Edwards*, vol. 21, ed. Harry S. Stout (New Haven, CT: Yale University Press, 2003), 113.
2. William Perkins, *A Golden Chaine* (Cambridge: John Legat, 1600), chap. 2.
3. John Frame, *Systematic Theology* (Philipsburg, NJ: P&R Publishing, 2013), 409.
4. William Walsham How, "We Give Thee But Thine Own," Hymnary.org, 1858, https://hymnary.org/text/we_give_thee_but_thine_own.
5. A. W. Tozer, *The Knowledge of the Holy* (New York: HarperCollins, 1961), 34.

CHAPTER 5: THE INCOMPREHENSIBLE GOD

1. Joel R. Beeke and Paul M. Smalley, *Reformed Systematic Theology: Revelation and God*, vol. 1 (Wheaton, IL: Crossway, 2019), 643.
2. A. W. Tozer, *The Knowledge of the Holy* (New York: HarperCollins, 1961), 8.
3. Thomas Boston, *An Illustration of the Doctrines of the Christian Religion with Respect to Faith and Practice upon the Plan of the Assembly's Shorter Catechism Comprehending a Complete Body of Divinity*, vol. 1 (Aberdeen, Scotland: George and Robert King, 1848), 80.

4. Matthew Barrett, *None Greater: The Undomesticated Attributes of God* (Grand Rapids: Baker Books, 2019), 18.

5. Attributed to Robert Keene, "How Firm a Foundation Ye Saints of the Lord," in John Rippon, *A Selection of Hymns* (London: Thomas Wilkins, 1787), 128.

6. Thomas Watson, *A Body of Divinity* (Edinburgh: The Banner of Truth Trust, 1983), 54.

CHAPTER 6: THE ALL-KNOWING, ALL-WISE GOD

1. I was helped by the way in which Rico Tice unfolded the drama of this scene in his exposition at the 2019 Basics Conference. See Rico Tice, "What Is Hidden Under Your Tent?," Basics Conference, May 6, 2019, https://www.truthforlife.org/resources/sermon/main-session-rico-tice.

CHAPTER 7: THE OMNIPRESENT GOD

1. R. C. Sproul, *Essential Truths of the Christian Faith* (Carol Stream, IL: Tyndale House Publishers, 1992), 296.

2. Stephen Charnock, *The Existence and Attributes of God* (Grand Rapids: Baker Books, 1996), 1:386, 1:398.

3. A. W. Tozer, *The Knowledge of the Holy* (New York: HarperCollins, 1961), 76.

4. See Matthew Barrett, *None Greater: The Undomesticated Attributes of God* (Grand Rapids: Baker Books, 2019), 182, who draws upon Augustine at this point.

CHAPTER 8: THE GLORIOUS GOD

1. Holly Hedegaard et al., "Increase in Suicide Mortality in the United States, 1999–2018," *NCHS Data Brief*, no. 362 (April 2020): 1–8, https://www.cdc.gov/nchs/data/databriefs/db362-h.pdf.

2. Clay Routledge, "Suicides Have Increased. Is This an Existential Crisis?," *New York Times*, June 23, 2018, https://www.nytimes.com/2018/06/23/opinion/sunday/suicide-rate-existential-crisis.html.

3. *The Shorter Catechism with Scripture Proofs* (Edinburgh: The Banner of Truth Trust, 2012), 5.

4. Saint Augustine, *Confessions*, trans. Henry Chadwick (Oxford: Oxford University Press, 2008), 3.

5. Harry Dixon Loes, "All Things in Jesus," Hymnary.org, 1915, https://hymnary.org/text/friends_all_around_us_are_trying_to_find.

6. See Timothy Keller, *Preaching: Communicating Faith in an Age of Skepticism* (New York: Viking, 2015), 107.

7. David Foster Wallace, "This Is Water," Farnam Street Media (blog), May 21, 2005, https://fs.blog/2012/04/david-foster-wallace-this-is-water.

E†T ENCOUNTER THE TRUTH

Encounter the Truth is the Bible teaching ministry of Jonathan Griffiths. Through faithful teaching of the Scriptures, we seek to facilitate encounters with the truth of God's Word—and ultimately, with the Lord Jesus Christ, who is the Truth that came down from heaven. Our prayer is that those who do not yet know Jesus will come to a saving knowledge of the truth, that believers will be grounded in the truth, and that local churches will be encouraged in their witness to the truth.

Programs can be heard on Moody Radio and other Christian radio stations in the United States and Canada, on multiple podcasting platforms, and through our website and app.

"WHAT IS GOD LIKE?"

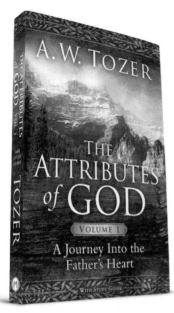

For A. W. Tozer, no question is more important than, "What is God like?" The desire to know God fueled his entire life and ministry.

This volume includes a study guide and sermons Tozer preached on ten attributes of God:

- Infinite
- Immense
- Good
- Just
- Merciful
- Gracious
- Omnipresent
- Immanent
- Holy
- Perfect

978-1-60066-129-7

also available as an eBook

Originally preached as sermons to the Avenue Road congregation in Toronto, this follow-up to *The Attributes of God Volume 1* examines ten more attributes of God. It also includes a study guide for an in-depth look at each attribute.

978-1-60066-138-9

also available as an eBook

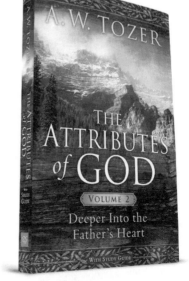

MOODY
Publishers®

From the Word **to Life**®